Illustrator:
Agnes S. Palinay

Editor:
Walter Kelly, M.A.

Senior Editor:
Sharon Coan, M.S. Ed.

Art Direction:
Elayne Roberts

Product Manager:
Phil Garcia

Imaging:
Alfred Lau

Cover Artist:
Blanca Apodaca La Bounty

Publishers:
Rachelle Cracchiolo, M.S. Ed.
Mary Dupuy Smith, M.S. Ed.

Interdisciplinary Unit

Freedom

CHALLENGING

Author:
Dona Herweck Rice

Teacher Created Materials, Inc.
P.O. Box 1040
Huntington Beach, CA   92647
ISBN-1-55734-606-2

©1994 Teacher Created Materials, Inc.   Made in U.S.A.

Table of Contents

Publication information and overseas availability appear on book pages.

Freedom Defined

Freedom seems a simple concept, but it is not simple to define. It is an idea, and as such, it has no shape, color, or size by which it may be categorized. Its definition depends on human sensibility.

Freedom is an internalized truth which we hope to have manifested in the outside world. When Martin Luther King, Jr. declared, "Free at last! Free at last! Thank God Almighty, we're free at last!" he did so with the understanding that freedom is the natural inheritance of all people and is, in fact, their rightful condition. Freedom is a fundamental right.

This is not to say that freedom exists universally. In many places and circumstances, freedom is evident only in its restriction or absence. Moreover, there is no system of government in existence today which maintains a *laissez faire* attitude toward freedom. In every nation, there are restrictions to freedom. For individuals, organizations, or political institutions in democracies such as the United States, such restrictions are set in order to protect the freedom of others. This, then, is freedom in its legal sense.

Freedom in its purest form is the absolute ability to make choices for oneself without restriction, and with the ample provision of all supporting information, time, and conditions. However, no formal society, no matter how supportive of freedom, exists without limitations on that freedom. Whether or not such a society *could* exist may prove a worthwhile topic for discussion or debate. Is it possible to trust individuals to their own discretion?

There are various kinds of freedom, and each is worth note. This book divides freedom into five component parts: intellectual, physical, political, social, and personal. Each part is investigated in depth through cross-curricular activities and one or two literature selections. If you are in a self-contained classroom (all subjects taught), you can satisfy all your curricular needs through this theme. If your classroom is content-centered (i.e., you are a language arts or social studies teacher) you may wish to take activities from other content areas and bring them to the attention of the other departments. You and the teachers of the other content areas might then work conjointly around the theme. Also, in some instances the activities for other content areas may be adapted to yours.

Before beginning any study of the component parts of freedom, it is advisable to define each for the class. Following is a brief description for each of the five freedoms listed previously.

Freedom Defined *(cont.)*

Intellectual Freedom:

Intellectual freedom is the opportunity to think and learn without restriction. This freedom suggests the possibility of exposure to everything that can be perceived intellectually, as well as the personal right to choose that to which one is exposed. There is great debate about the value of this type of freedom for young people. Are they helped or hindered by it? Should this freedom be limited?

Physical Freedom:

Physical freedom is the limitless opportunity to move. When one is physically free, one can come and go as one pleases when one pleases. There are no restrictions to physical motion. Yet, there is no place in the world where physical freedom is without limit. Are there any sensible reasons for this to be so?

Political Freedom:

Political freedom is the opportunity of all people to take part in the governmental decision-making process. Politically free people have a voice which is heard and counts. Their opinions are expressed and their needs addressed. Decisions for the whole are made by the whole. What rights do people in politically free societies have?

Social Freedom:

Social freedom is the opportunity to live, worship, speak, work, and interrelate as one chooses. Cultural expression in a multicultural society finds its voice here. Given social freedom, each person has the right to be exactly who he/she is. Can individuals be themselves without infringing on the rights of others?

Personal Freedom:

This freedom is most precious of all, for it provides the unrestricted space and leisure to know oneself. Under this premise, every individual has free reign to learn and grow, developing the seed of who he/she really is (or can become). There are no internal restrictions on that awareness, and no external forces moving to prohibit an individual's discovery. Personal freedom suggests personal peace.

Yet psychologically speaking, the human mind has natural defenses (such as denial or disassociation) that sometimes protect individuals from conscious awareness. What might be some reasons for the existence of these defenses?

Preparing Your Classroom

Bulletin Board

As a class, brainstorm words that mean or suggest "freedom" (some words are suggested below). Have individual students each choose a word, and then write that word in large, open-style type. Each student will then color/decorate the word. Display all the decorated words under the heading "Freedom" (also decorated). Collage the words with photocopied, photographed, or illustrated images of freedom. (You might also include the activity from page 6.) This display will be a productive springboard for numerous writing, social studies, and history activities. Please make sure that all students have the freedom to participate in the preparation of the bulletin board.

Freedom Words

Use these words for the bulletin board above, display them around your classroom, or have each student draw one from a hat and freewrite a response to the word.

- liberty
- independence
- emancipation
- permission
- immunity
- license
- release
- elbow room
- exemption

Classroom Arrangement

Rearrange the classroom in a way determined and voted on by the students and yourself. Allow for the expression of all ideas, and the free vote of each individual. Be sure to follow through on the group consensus. As an additional way to demonstrate freedom, teach class out-of-doors one day per week—with the weather's cooperation, of course.

If you choose, you can use the division pages for each section on freedom in this book to color and display around your classroom.

Poetry Display

Around the room or in an especially designated nook, display multicultural poems and songs that celebrate freedom. If any students are willing, have them illustrate the poems for display. Here are some suggested anthologies that each contain a number of poems/songs appropriate to the theme.

Bryan, Ashley, ed. *All Night, All Day: A Child's First Book of African-American Spirituals.* (Atheneum, 1991)

Hughes, Langston. *Selected Poems of Langston Hughes.* (Vintage, 1990)

Nye, Naomi Shihab, ed. *This Same Sky: A Collection of Poems from Around the World.* (Four Winds Press, 1992)

Sneve, Virginia Driving Hawk, ed. *Dancing Teepees.* (Holiday House, 1989)

Soto, Gary. *A Fire in My Hands.* (Scholastic, 1990)

What Is Freedom?

Name: _____ Date: _____

Somewhere inside you is the little child of four, five, or six that you used to be. That little child knew (and still knows) how to color and draw for pleasure. It does not matter to him or her what the picture looks like to other people. Most important is what it represents for that small child.

To do this activity, you will need a box of crayons. Sit or lie down somewhere by yourself, and on the back of this paper, color what freedom means to you. (Of course, freedom itself suggests that you can get an entirely different piece of paper if you wish.) There are no rules or guidelines for this. Your drawing can be anything you would like.

When you are finished, give your picture a title and write it here. Under the title, freewrite* your explanation of/response to your picture.

Freewriting means you write down your ideas when they come to you, exactly *as* they come to you. When you freewrite, you write down whatever is in your head without stopping to look up spelling in the dictionary, correct your grammar, or change your sentence structure.

_____
(picture title)

Intellectual Freedom

The Opportunity to Think and Learn Without Restriction

Name: _____ Date: _____

Poetry

Poetry conveys feelings and ideas through carefully constructed images. It is meant to be personal. Its meaning depends on both the poem and the individual reader.

Read the following poem. On the back of this page write what you think the poem means. As a class, share and discuss your opinions.

Bubbles in the Air

A playful flash across
Two round blue eyes
. . . and a giggle.
Then pucker,
Blow . . .
A silent spray of soapy drops
Out and down
Splashes the grass below.

The child laughs.

"Again," her eyes say.
Steady the wand . . .
Tiny lips round,
Then, hinting a smile
Blow once more.
Droplets scatter.
But eyes dance,
Oblivious to defeat,
Delighted by the process.

Wordless she teaches.

And her laughter floats
Like bubbles in the air.

— *Dona Herweck Rice*

Name: _____ Date: _____

Speeches

Perhaps the most famous speech on freedom ever given was by Martin Luther King, Jr. at the March on Washington in August of 1963. Thousands listened as King spoke their common hope for a world united in love, peace, and acceptance, where each individual is free to be, think, and do as he/she wishes. The air resounded that day with King's impassioned cry of freedom at last for all people.

Part of the power behind the speech was King's strong feelings about the subject. He believed vehemently in freedom and peace for all people. Perhaps you feel as strongly as King did. Then again, maybe your passion is for a different cause, like health care for all people, an answer to homelessness, a cure for AIDS, or any number of other concerns in our world today.

Choose an issue or topic about which you feel strongly (it may be one of the above). Below, brainstorm your feelings about it. Why is it important? What can we do about it? Next, take the information you brainstormed and, on the reverse, gather the information to outline a persuasive speech on the topic of your choice. From the outline, draft a speech. If you have chosen a topic close to your heart, the words will likely come easily to you.

_____
Topic

Why Is It Important?   **What Can We Do About It?**

_____   _____

_____   _____

_____   _____

_____   _____

_____   _____

_____   _____

_____   _____

_____   _____

Name: _____ Date: _____

Communication

A lot of freedom comes from the ability to express what you know clearly and intelligently. Sometimes a person simply needs to think first before speaking; then knowledge has the chance to take shape in intelligent communication. Try the two activities below to illustrate this idea.

Giving Directions

Choose one item from the list below this paragraph. Write careful, specific directions on how to do the activity you have chosen. When you have finished, look over your directions again. Make sure that you have been as clear as you can. Do not title your directions.

- tying your shoes
- doing a somersault
- snapping your fingers
- jumping on one foot
- making a book cover
- folding a paper airplane

Now, exchange directions with someone else. Each person will then follow the directions he/she was given. Do this in front of the class or in small groups. See how many sets of directions were clear. Were important bits of information left out?

It's a Draw

On any scrap of paper, draw some sort of geometric object. Your object needs to include at least three shapes. Here are some ideas:

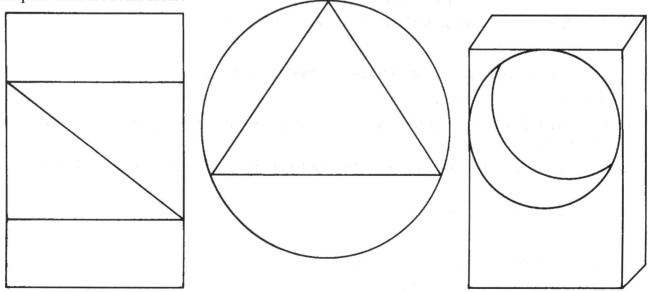

Now, pick a partner. Don't show each other your drawings. Sit back to back. One at a time, give oral directions for drawing your object. How well do your two drawings match up?

Holidays

Holidays are something that people the world over have in common. However, not all holidays are common to all people. The freedom to know about holidays from other cultures—and even to honor and celebrate them—is every person's intellectual and social right.

Below, you will find a partial list of holidays from various cultures. From this list choose one that you know *nothing* about. Research it to find what that holiday is, the reason(s) for celebrating it, and at least one traditional custom associated with it. Share this information with your class.

Arbor Day, April Fool's Day, Anzac Day, Ash Wednesday, Advent, Admissions Day, Australia Day, Armistice Day

Bastille Day, Buddha's Birthday, Boxing Day, Bonfire Night

Children's Day, Chinese New Year, Christmas, Cinco de Mayo, Canada Day, Ch'usok, Candlemas Day

Day of the Dead, Doll's Festival, Divali

Easter, Epiphany

Friendship Day, Father's Day, Flag Day, Feast of Hungry Ghosts, Feast of St. Nicholas

Ground Hog Day, Guy Fawkes Day, Good Friday, Guadalupe Day

Halloween, Hanukkah, Hogmanay

Independence Day

Jean Baptiste Day

Kwanzaa, Kamehameha Day

Labor Day, Lent, Leif Ericson Day, Lincoln's Birthday

Martin Luther King, Jr. Day, Mother's Day, May Day, Mardi Gras, Memorial Day, Muhammad's Birthday, Moomba Festival, Maundy Thursday, Midsummer Day

New Year's Eve, New Year's Day, Navajo Nation Fair, National Day

Oktoberfest, Olympic games

President's Day, Purim, Pancake Day, Passover, Patriot's Day, Pulaski Day

Quinceaños, Quebec National Day

Rosh Hashanah, Ramadan, Remembrance Day, Robert E. Lee's Birthday, Republic Day, Rondy, Rizal Day

St. Patrick's Day, St. Lucia Day, Simon Bolivar's Birthday, Shichi-Go-San, Susan B. Anthony Day, Shabuot

Thanksgiving, Tanabata Matsuri

United Nations Day

Valentine's Day, Veteran's Day, Victoria Day

Washington's Birthday, Waitangi Day

Yom Kippur

Name: _____ Date: _____

Algebra

The more math a person knows, the more intellectually free that person is to use his/her mind to its potential. Yet, since the first school began, students by the thousands have repeated the same question: "When am I ever gonna need this?" The answer is simple. Though you may not need to know a specific equation, the logical growth you stimulate from solving that equation has the same effect as running up to a few brain cells and permanently shaking them awake! Now, with that in mind, welcome to the world of—ALGEBRA!

Algebra is a branch of mathematics that helps us solve for unknown sets or values. The unknowns are often represented in an equation with x. With algebra, many problems can be solved that simple arithmetic alone cannot solve.

The problems at the bottom of this page are basic algebra. X is the unknown. You must find the value of x in each problem. To do so, take the *whole number* on the left of the equal sign and subtract it from (1) itself, and then (2) the number on the right of the equal sign. Now you are left with "x =" and a number that tells you the value of x. For example:

A. $x + 3 = 7$

   $(x + 3) - 3 = 7 - 3$

   $x = 4$

B. $x + 9 = 12$

   $(x + 9) - 9 = 12 - 9$

   $x = 3$

If you substitute each value for x into the original problems, you will see that the answer for each is correct. In sample A "3+4 = 7" is true, and in sample B "9+3 = 12" is also true.

Now, do the following problems yourself.

1. $x + 6 = 29$

2. $x + 9 = 17$

3. $x + 1 = 83$

4. $x + 32 = 94$

5. $x + 101 = 102$

6. $x + 26 = 26$

7. $x + 18 = 1,008$

8. $x + 3 = 10$

9. $x + 56 = 79$

10. $x + 76 = 324$

Name: _____ Date: _____

Logic

Test your intellectual process with logic. Logical development frees your mind to think analytically, a skill called for again and again in life. You can use your math skills and your power of reason to solve the logic puzzle below.

1. Zachary lives in the first house.

2. Alicia lives three houses after Zachary.

3. Nicholas is five years older than Zachary.

4. Kenny is two years younger than Nicholas.

5. Travis lives in the last house on the block.

6. Brianna is four years younger than the oldest child.

7. Alicia is older than Kenny.

8. Kenny lives one house past (after) Alicia.

9. Brianna lives three houses before Travis.

Age	First House	Second House	Third House	Fourth House	Fifth House	Sixth House
One						
Two						
Three						
Four						
Five						
Six						

Finding Out Why and How

Intellectual freedom is crucial to the scientist. Without the freedom to question, examine, study, and learn, nothing new can be discovered and no answers can be found. Use your intellectual freedom to investigate one of the problems below. Choose one that you do not already know.

1. Why does water run through pipes to your faucet?

2. How does a refrigerator keep food cold?

3. Why do flowers have a sweet scent?

4. Why do fingernails grow?

5. Why do people have different color eyes? Who or what decides what color a baby's eyes will be?

6. Why do some people have freckles?

7. Why does it rain a lot in some places and very little in others?

8. Does solar energy work on a cloudy day?

9. How does gasoline run the average car?

10. Why do people need to eat? What makes them get hungry?

11. Why do earthquakes often occur in coastal areas?

12. Why don't giant redwoods grow in the tropical rain forests?

13. Why do dogs make good pets but wolves do not?

14. Why does it take longer for sugar to dissolve in cold water than in hot?

15. Why can fish live underwater but humans cannot?

The Scientific Method

The "scientific method" is an outline for conducting scientific experiments. Whenever a scientist wishes to test a hypothesis, he/she follows this procedure and carefully studies the results. A good scientist tests many hypotheses, some of them repeatedly, in order to draw accurate and sound conclusions.

Whenever conducting your own experiment, use the following form. Here is your first challenge:

From five different frozen liquids, which one will melt the quickest and which one will melt the slowest? You may use any five liquids. For example, you may try tap water, saltwater, lemon juice, milk, and soda pop.

Scientist:_____

Name of Experiment: _____

Question: What am I trying to find out?

_____

_____

Hypothesis: What do I think will happen?

_____

_____

_____

Procedure: How will I go about doing this?

_____

_____

_____

Results: What happened?

_____

_____

_____

Conclusion: What did I find out?

_____

_____

_____

_____

_____

Name: _____ Date: _____

Modern Art

Artists throughout time have been in perpetual motion. They have moved from medium to medium, form to form, to further their possibilities for creative expression. In the 20th century, the world of art has known cubism, dadaism, photorealism, pointillism, surrealism, and more. Pollock, Matisse, Picasso, and others have challenged our perspective and intellectual tolerance. The person resistant to change and novelty sees only that Pollock "threw paint," Matisse "cut paper," and Picasso "drew like a child." Yet these giants of the art world were truly on the artistic frontier, ever exploring and pushing their own limits. They were masters of traditional form, yet so much more.

Canvas and paint are common mediums for the artist. Now it is time to challenge your own limits to uncover other possibilities. Add to the following lists whatever materials and surfaces come to mind. Include both the typical and the unusual. Let your imagination soar. Use the back of this paper if you need more room.

Materials	Surfaces
paint	canvas
crayons	mirrors
lipstick	paper
_____	_____
_____	_____
_____	_____
_____	_____
_____	_____
_____	_____
_____	_____
_____	_____
_____	_____

Name: _____ Date: _____

Modern Art II

On the previous page, you found many new mediums by which works of art may be created. Keeping in mind that the primary purpose of art is to express yourself, not to please others, choose mediums from your list that appeal to you. You are going to create your own artwork.

Now that you have your mediums, you will need a subject. (Perhaps you will wish to choose your subject first and *then* your medium. That is all right, too.) To decide upon a subject, a good way to begin is to get in touch with your feelings right now. Art and feelings are both creative, and therefore they work hand-in-hand. Read over the list of feelings below, and circle any that appeal to you now.

afraid	embarrassed	overwhelmed
angry	enraged	peaceful
anxious	exhausted	playful
apprehensive	frightened	puzzled
ashamed	frustrated	sad
bewildered	guilty	serene
bored	happy	shocked
calm	hopeful	shy
cautious	hysterical	silly
clumsy	jealous	smug
confident	joyful	surprised
confused	lonely	suspicious
depressed	lovesick	terrified
disgusted	lovestruck	tired
ecstatic	quarrelsome	uptight
edgy	mischievous	worried

Let your art be an extension of the feelings you selected. On the back of this page, brainstorm subjects that fit your feeling description. The subjects must come entirely from you. Although a subject calls forth a certain feeling for you, it may call forth a different response from someone else.

Finally, create your work of art using the mediums, feeling(s), and subject(s) you've chosen. Remember, art is for your own expression! You don't have to please anyone else.

Designing an Instrument

Musical instruments are divided into five main classes: (1) stringed, (2) wind, (3) percussion, (4) keyboard, and (5) electronic. *Stringed instruments* produce sound when the musician makes the strings vibrate, either by plucking them or by using a bow. They include violins, guitars, harps, and cellos, among others. *Wind instruments* make sound when the musician blows into or through a tube. These instruments are either woods or brass, and they include trumpets, bugles, clarinets, flutes, and more. *Percussion instruments* create their sound by being shaken or hit with sticks. They include drums, symbols, tambourines, triangles, and others. *Keyboards* are played by pressing keys that are attached to sound-making devices. Keyboards are easy to identify, and they include pianos, organs, and harpsichords. *Electronic instruments* either create, amplify, or reproduce sound through electricity. The electric guitar, electric piano, and synthesizer are the most popular electric instruments.

Instruments have evolved over time. Someone first has an idea, someone else sees it a different way, someone else builds upon it, and so forth. But remember, *first* someone has the idea.

Below you will find a list of common household materials. Collect any of the materials you can, as well as any others you would like to add, and with them design an instrument of your very own. Your instrument can be a new approach to an old design or a completely new piece. You decide! You have the freedom to choose.

- cardboard tubes (from towels and toilet paper)
- aluminum foil
- plastic wrap
- waxed paper
- rubber bands
- twine
- paper plates, bowls, and cups
- wooden spoons
- plastic bags
- paper bags
- glass jars of different sizes
- plastic containers of different sizes
- shoe boxes
- newspapers
- old tins and utensils

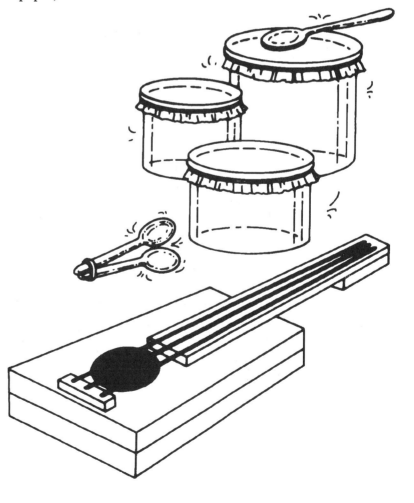

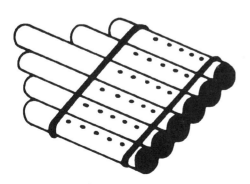

Rewriting an Old Song

Children have always loved to change the words to familiar songs. During the winter holidays, how many children have been known to choose "Jingle Bells, Batman Smells" over the traditional version? Or how about "On Top of Spaghetti"? Songs like that are often silly and always a lot of fun.

Once you get the hang of it, rewriting songs is easy to do. The key is to match up the new words to the old. Syllable count is important if you want to be able to sing the song smoothly and easily. For example, "On Top of Old Smoky" and "On Top of Spaghetti" match up, syllable for syllable. Some of the words of the original song are left in, too. This makes the song recognizable for others as an imitation.

Following are two original samples. Try them for fun, and use them as models, if you wish, to create your own.

In My Room

(sung to the tune of "Dixie")

Oh, I wish I were in my house a-sleepin'
Out this door I should be creepin'
Home again! Home again! Home again, in my room!

Oh, I wish I were a-sleepin'! Hooray! Hooray!
A-sleepin's where I want to be
Away back home in my room!

Yip-Yap, Yip-Yap, Little Dog

(sung to the tune of "Twinkle, Twinkle, Little Star")

Yip-yap, yip-yap, little dog,
How I wish I'd bought a frog.
All the night you yip and yap.
How do you make noise like that?
Yip-yap, yip-yap, little dog,
How I wish I'd bought a frog.

Making a New Recipe

Creativity is one of the best side effects of intellectual freedom. This freedom opens a person to experimentation, because if a person is free, then he/she can choose for himself what to think and do. Most importantly, true intellectual freedom supports a person in both success *and* failure, because there is self-acceptance either way.

An intellectually free person is always willing to try new ideas. In fact, this person is willing to risk coming up with his/her own ideas. Here is a fun way to challenge your own intellectual freedom.

Written below is a list of various ingredients that can be found in any number of dishes. From this list, as well as from your own ideas, choose any ingredients that appeal to you for the creation of an all-new recipe. You can make a dessert, main dish, vegetable dish, salad, bread—anything at all. Just make it different. Make it your own. There is only one restriction—you must be willing to sample your own creation.

plums	apples	sugar	salt
carrots	tortillas	jack cheese	pepper
mustard	carrots	chicken	pineapple
red peppers	vanilla	corn meal	bean sprouts
green peppers	whipped cream	buttermilk	yogurt
pears	eggs	flour	syrup
pretzels	bananas	margarine	oranges
ketchup	potatoes	chocolate	spinach
lemons	olive oil	pepperoni	soy sauce
yeast	cheddar cheese	graham crackers	olives
butter	rice	milk	corn
brown sugar	applesauce	strawberries	onions
raisins	tomatoes	peppermint	peaches
cranberries	navy beans	mushrooms	peanut butter
dates	cottage cheese	mozzarella cheese	pepper sauce
water	jelly	pasta	peas
cinnamon	mayonnaise	wheat bread	broccoli
mayonnaise	macaroni	ground beef	asparagus
blueberries	cantaloupe	tuna fish	cherries
limes	string beans	potato chips	garlic powder

Name: _____ Date: _____

Thinking for Yourself

Often we spend so much time thinking about others and what they think of us, that we forget to look at ourselves and listen to what we think. Here is your chance to get to know yourself a little better.

Respond to the following situations with your own opinions and ideas. Write down only what feels right to you, not what you think you are supposed to write or what someone else wants you to write. Be honest. Afterward, you can discuss your ideas as a class, or keep them to yourself if you choose.

A.   You stayed late after school, so as you walk home it is getting dark. You are not sure, but you think someone is following you. You are frightened. What do you do?

   _____

   _____

B.   You have just gone to the mall with your brother/sister. He/she is two years older than you. You are concerned because, while shopping, you think he/she stole something valuable from a department store display. What do you do?

   _____

   _____

C.   You are playing football with a friend. Your friend injures another player. Everyone is sure it was an accident, but you know it was on purpose. What do you do?

   _____

   _____

D.   Another student has been threatening you. This student has told you that unless you pay a protection fee every week, you will be hurt. What do you do?

   _____

   _____

E.   Your teacher assigned you an essay due tomorrow. It is an important part of your grade. However, you have been working on a special project at home that is very important to you. You know you can finish it tonight if you have no other interruptions. What do you do?

   _____

   _____

F.   You are angry at one of your parents. He/she hurt your feelings. It was unintentional, but still you were hurt and you want an apology. What do you do?

   _____

   _____

Name: _____ Date: _____

A New Game

You have been hired by the Olympic committee to create a new game for special exhibition at the next Olympics. The guidelines they have given are as follows:

- Use a soccer ball.
- Play on a basketball court.
- Have three teams play at once.
- Give each team four players.

Your job is to make the strategy and rules for this new game. How do you play? What is it called? Draw the set-up of the game here. Write the rules and strategy on the back. If you are really ambitious, design a uniform, too.

The Mind/Body Connection

Body Language

Everyone has feelings. They are normal and natural. However, when a person chooses not to acknowledge or express his/her feelings, the energy behind that feeling is still carried somewhere in the body. People throughout time have known this to be true. Common language reflects it. In the English language, there are phrases that clearly show the mind/body connection. For example, when a person is frustrated by someone else, that person says that the other is "a pain in the neck." If one person is feeling nagged by another, that person says that the other person is "on my back." Or, if someone feels controlled by someone else—either out of love or fear—that person may say that the other "has a hold on me."

In small groups or as a class, brainstorm other common phrases in the language that show the mind/body connection.

Feeling Feelings

Take a look at the list of feelings from page 17. Choose any ten feelings. For each, write down the place in your body where you feel it. For example, anger might be felt in the chest, stomach, or shoulders, or joy might be felt in the heart. Though people are similar, feeling sensations are not the same for everyone, so your answers are fine as long as they are true for you. (Note: If you are not sure how you feel about something, often your body will tell you if you pay attention to its signals.)

Relieving Stress

Whenever a person is feeling under stress, that person frequently tenses his/her muscles. As a result, his/her neck, shoulders, back, and head get tight and painful. In small groups or as a class, brainstorm things to do before tension causes body aches in a stressful situation. Then, brainstorm things to do after the aches arrive.

Peaceful Pictures

Close your eyes and imagine the most beautiful place you can. See all of its colors. Imagine how it smells. Are there any people there? Are there buildings? Describe them. Is it a natural setting or man-made (or both)? Look it over every way you can. Now, put yourself in the middle of it.

Whenever you feel tense, lonely, or frustrated, close your eyes and go back to your peaceful picture. You are sure to feel better in every way.

The Day They Came to Arrest the Book

by Nat Hentoff (Dell, 1983)

(Available in Canada, Dell; UK, Penguin; Australia, Transworld Publishers)

Summary: Principal Mike Moore opens the doors of George Mason High School for a new school year. Barney Roth, a junior and editor of the school paper, returns to school ready for the challenges the year will hold. Yet, almost immediately he and his peers meet with one of the most controversial experiences of their lives. It involves the banning of books, and it begins with one of the students themselves.

The reader learns from the outset that Mr. Moore is a shady character, *shady* being a key word here because the principal prefers to act in secrecy, behind closed doors. There is a suggestion that the school's former librarian has left under some sort of duress. The reader must wait for the specifics. Meanwhile, the new controversy brews. Asserting that the book is racist, one student, Gordon McLean, strongly objects to the required reading of *The Adventures of Huckleberry Finn* in his history class, taught by Nora Baines. Gordon's father insists that Mr. Moore remove the book from the school entirely. The principal is willing, but his actions are halted by Miss Baines and the new librarian, Deirdre Fitzgerald. They insist that he follow pre-determined procedures for handling citizen complaints and challenges. As the situation becomes public, others join the fight against the book, adding the accusations of sexism and immorality as reasons it should be banned.

Barney, Nora, and Deirdre embark on a battle to preserve the freedoms of the First Amendment. They are eloquent, but so are those in opposition, namely Matthew Griswold, a charming intellectual who represents the Citizens' League for the Preservation of American Values. Mr. Griswold is skilled in the art of manipulation, shaming individuals into his perspective, all the while seeming very rational, calm, and pleasant. Miss Baines is hardly more admirable to the reader, for though her cause is just, she uses anger and personal attacks to fight for her position. Shining above it all is the new librarian, intelligent and strong, open to the free airing of viewpoints other than her own, for that is how she protects the very freedom for which she is fighting. Barney, too, proves his intelligence, working within the system to fight it.

At the most crucial moment, the former librarian, Karen Salters, comes forward with her story. For two years she was made to remove books from the shelves of the library through the coercion of Mr. Moore. When finally she challenged him by threatening exposure to his behind-the-scenes manipulations, he proceeded to make her employment at the school so unbearable that she had to leave for her own peace of mind. It seems Mr. Moore had even ripped pages from books (including the Bible) in attempts to censor! Barney prints Mrs. Salters' story in the school paper.

The situation escalates from this point to the local and then national media. The resulting publicity sways the vote in favor of the First Amendment; the book is freed. However, the novel ends ominously. We close on Mr. Moore who is in a celebrational mood, quite sure that having won, the proponents of printed freedom will now rest easily, and he and the other censors will have free rein to move in and reelect a board more favorable to their ideas. The point is clear. Part of freedom is the responsibility to preserve that freedom. It carries with it the inherent threat that anyone, anytime, can and will try to take it away.

Commonly Censored Books and Plays

The following list of books and plays are among those most commonly censored in the western world.

- *The Adventures of Huckleberry Finn* by Mark Twain
- *Black Boy* by Richard Wright
- *Brave New World* by Aldous Huxley
- *Catch-22* by Joseph Heller
- *The Catcher in the Rye* by J.D. Salinger
- *The Chocolate War* by Robert Cormier
- *The Crucible* by Arthur Miller
- *A Farewell to Arms* by Ernest Hemingway
- *The Glass Menagerie* by Tennessee Williams
- *Go Ask Alice* (Anonymous)
- *The Great Gatsby* by F. Scott Fitzgerald
- *A Hero Ain't Nothin' but a Sandwich* by Alice Childress
- *I Know Why the Caged Bird Sings* by Maya Angelou
- *The Lion, the Witch and the Wardrobe* by C.S. Lewis
- *Lord of the Flies* by William Golding
- *1984* by George Orwell
- *Of Mice and Men* by John Steinbeck
- *Our Town* by Thorton Wilder
- *The Outsiders* by S.E. Hinton
- *The Pigman* by Paul Zindel
- *Slaughterhouse Five* by Kurt Vonnegut
- *The Slave Dancer* by Paula Fox
- *Then Again, Maybe I Won't* by Judy Blume
- *To Kill a Mockingbird* by Harper Lee
- *The Wizard of Oz* by L. Frank Baum

Choose any one of the books from the above list. Read it yourself. In one page, write your honest response to the book. How did it make you feel? Did it challenge you to look at anything in a new way? What effect did it have on you? Do you think this book deserves to be censored, and if so, for what reason(s)?

Now, research at least two reviews or commentaries on the book. How are the perspectives there like or unlike your own?

Note: For more information on censored materials and works currently being censored, read the *Newsletter on Intellectual Freedom* published by the American Library Association.

Name: _____ Date: _____

Anthony Comstock

In the early 1870's, a man named Anthony Comstock began a crusade against the publication, distribution, and reading of certain materials which he deemed morally reprehensible and responsible for criminal activity in the country's youth.

Comstock was born to a highly religious family. His righteous beliefs were supported to such a degree that even before he turned eighteen, he took it upon himself to raid a local saloon, "driving out" the corruption he found there. In 1871, his focus of attention continued to be the local saloons, where he found a particular need to report them for non-adherence to the Sunday Closing Laws. In 1872, he banded with three other men, each prominent in society, to found the Society for the Suppression of Vice in New York. The following year, Comstock travelled to Washington, D.C., to lobby for a federal statute against the inclusion of obscenity or information about birth control and abortion in materials that are delivered through the mail. This became known as the Comstock Law. In 1873, Comstock was appointed Special Agent of the Postmaster General, a position he held without pay until 1906, to act as watchdog over his new law. The law itself has yet to be challenged at the Supreme Court level, and therefore it is law even today. It is widely believed that should there come a time when the Supreme Court must pass judgment on the law, it would be found in violation of the First Amendment to the U.S. Constitution.

Like many of his targets, Comstock was a writer. His most popular book was *Traps for the Young* (1883). The traps to which Comstock refers are numerous. They include advertisements, literature through the mail, dime novels, playing pool, contraceptives, smoking, saloons, much classic literature, and the fine arts. Comstock believed that these things were the direct cause of corruption in the country's youth and the rampant crime found among them. The destruction of these "evils" was his life's work.

During the course of his lifetime, Anthony Comstock was associated with the legal arraignment of over 3,800 people, the conviction or guilty plea of more than 2,800 people, $237,134.30 in fines, and prison terms totalling 565 years, 11 months, and 20 days. His actions have also been linked to 15 suicides. Comstock himself died in 1915.

Respond:

What do you think of the work of Anthony Comstock? Was he in the right? Do you support his actions? Write your response in freewrite style. Use the back of this paper for more room. Then discuss your ideas with the class.

My Reactions to Anthony Comstock's Work

_____

_____

_____

_____

_____

The American Civil Liberties Union

The American Civil Liberties Union (ACLU) is a nonpartisan organization founded in 1920 for the primary purpose of protecting and defending individual and group rights as guaranteed by the Constitution of the United States. It consists of approximately 300,000 members who fight for the freedoms of all people.

The ACLU works to provide legal services and lawyers for individuals or groups at local, state, and federal levels. Some of the causes, both present and past, of the ACLU are the following:

- separation of church and state
- desegregation of schools
- civil rights
- legal aid to the poor
- abolition of capital punishment
- abortion

- restriction of governmental agencies of investigation
- the rights of conscientious objectors
- the right of all groups to march and demonstrate
- the rights of homosexuals
- the rights of immigrants
- the rights of the mentally ill

Nat Hentoff includes the character of Kent Dickinson in his novel, *The Day They Came to Arrest the Book*. Mr. Dickinson is a young lawyer with the ACLU, quite comfortable (though somewhat clumsy) in his support of the First Amendment. His arguments are sound and completely in keeping with the tenor of the amendment. His character acts as the voice of the Constitution in the novel.

Choose one of the issues listed above as causes for the ACLU. Write a logical and concise argument stating your point of view on that issue. Then, as a class, join together by issue selected and share the differing points of view offered.

_____

_____

_____

_____

_____

_____

_____

_____

_____

_____

_____

Note: To contact the ACLU directly, write to its headquarters at 132 West 43rd Street, New York, NY 10036.

Name: _____ Date: _____

The First Amendment and Censorship

Following is the First Amendment (adopted 1791) to the Constitution of the United States:

"Congress shall make no law respecting an establishment of religion, or prohibiting the free exercise thereof; or abridging the freedom of speech, or of the press; or the right of the people peaceably to assemble, and to petition the government for a redress of grievances."

This amendment is said to hold the five basic freedoms: **religion, speech, press, assembly,** and **petition.** Read the amendment carefully and then read it again. Understand what it is saying.

Now, argue for or against censorship, using the First Amendment in defense of your argument.

Does the amendment support censorship or deny it? Write your response here.

_____

_____

_____

_____

_____

_____

_____

_____

_____

_____

_____

_____

_____

_____

_____

When completed, share your ideas with the class. Discuss the First Amendment with one another. Is there a class consensus on censorship and the First Amendment?

Challenge:

Find modern day incidents involving the protection of the First Amendment. For example, recently the right to burn the American flag as a political statement has been challenged. Find other such incidents and then discuss them.

Name: _____ Date: _____

Common Reasons to Censor

There are many reasons why people feel a need to censor the information and ideas available to others. Though their right to do so seems always in question, the fact that people do censor is obvious. The papers are filled with situations where one individual or group wishes to restrict the information available to others through various means and levels of legislation.

The reasons for such censoring are many. They include the following:

- sexual indecency
- non-patriotism
- secular humanism
- pacifism
- anti-religion
- promotion of civil rights
- offensive language
- discussion of drugs
- inappropriate adolescent behavior

- homosexual activity
- poor grammar
- sexism
- defamation of historic leaders
- multicultural and cultural distinctions
- lack of cultural distinctions
- violence
- immorality

This list can go on and on. It seems safe to say that no matter what the printed matter, there is someone, somewhere, who finds it offensive, and still more who would like to see it censored.

In an effort to match the above list of reasons for censoring, brainstorm here all the reasons not to censor.

_____

_____

_____

_____

_____

In the list above of reasons to censor, are there any arguments you support? In short, do you believe there is a reason worthy of promoting censorship? If so, tell your reason here. You have a right to your opinion!

_____

_____

_____

_____

_____

_____

Editorials

Editorials are opinion-based articles found in newspapers and some other periodicals. To write one, an editor takes an issue, often of some controversy, and adopts a strong standpoint upon which to argue. He/she substantiates that point of view with facts, statistics, and the corresponding opinions of authorities on the subject. Editorials are often meant to persuade the reader to adopt the editor's opinion.

When a person gives opinion in any writing, often it is said that the individual is editorializing. Sometimes these opinions are tucked inside an otherwise objective article, and while some consider that style of writing good journalism, others will call it inappropriate and even deceptive.

There are three types of editorials. The *unsigned editorial* reflects the opinion of the newspaper as a whole. One can usually assume that this editorial was written by the editor-in-chief of the paper. These editorials are often prominently featured. The *signed editorial* strictly reflects the opinion of the author. It may also be prominently featured, and usually it does not sway far from the overall opinion and perspective of the paper as a whole. *Letters-to-the-editor* are the third type of editorial. Anyone may write them, but it is up to the editorial staff of the newspaper to determine which are actually printed. Often these letters come in response to something already published in the newspaper. Other times they reflect an individual's concern over the state of some situation in public life, either locally, nationwide, or internationally.

Read the editorial section of your local newspaper. (If your family does not subscribe to one, copies may usually be read at your local library.) Find an editorial that strikes a chord with you, either of agreement or disagreement. Write a letter-to-the-editor in response to what you read. Send it to the newspaper (the address will likely be found in the "letters" section). To write a letter, follow these three steps:

1. Introduce the issue and give your opinion.

2. List any factual or authoritative support you have.

3. Summarize your opinion, adding persuasive arguments as to why the reader would benefit by adopting your opinion.

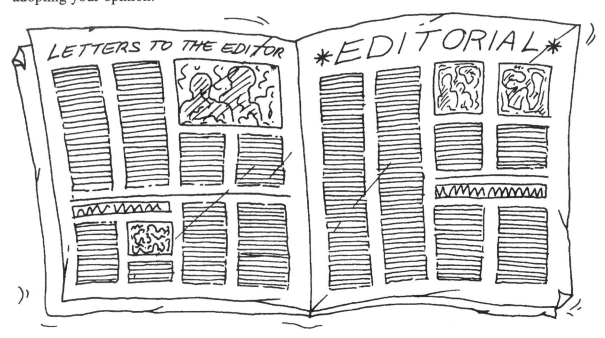

"The Censors Can't Stand Light"

Censors are oftentimes groups or individuals who simply want everyone else to think, feel, and react as they do. Though individuals wishing to sway others to their opinions sometimes use logical arguments to do so (and then allow others to make up their own minds), far more frequently people wishing to persuade others use manipulative tactics. They include shame, secrecy, lies, and fear. All of these tactics are in evidence in *The Day They Came to Arrest the Book*.

Shame is an emotion that everyone has, but a manipulator uses it to coerce others into doing and thinking as he/she wishes. Mike Moore uses shame every time he says, "I'm sure you agree," or "I'm sure you feel…" These statements covertly—though clearly—give the message that, should the hearer have a different opinion, he or she is quite foolish. There is no freedom to think in any way but as the speaker dictates *unless* the hearer wishes to appear unwise. The speaker has attempted to show (through the threat of shame) that there is, in fact, only one opinion worth consideration. Others are not even worth mention.

Secrecy is what Nora Baines refers to when she makes the statement, "The censors can't stand light." Because censorship robs others of their right to know, it is often done just as any other robbery, in secrecy. Censors want to control, and going public may mean a challenge to their control. The easier way—the controlled way—is behind closed doors. Mighty Mike illustrates this well by ripping out pages from books. He becomes a vandal and a thief to support his cause.

Lies, in both the forms of half truths and complete deception, are another prime tool of the censor. Again, when the point is to control, an individual may have no qualms about going to whatever means necessary to do so. Principal Moore demonstrates this well before the television cameras. His allusions communicate to the viewer that Karen Salters is somehow imbalanced and that she regrets any untruths she spread. Which brings up an extended tool of the censor who lies: turning the guilt onto the parties he/she is trying to control.

Fear, the fourth tool of the censor, is practiced by the principal in nearly every private encounter he has with an individual who stands in his way. Because she is afraid for her job and livelihood, Karen Salters does not act as her conscience dictates. This threat is not imagined. Covertly and overtly it has been made clear to her.

However, Karen Salters is also an example of an individual who rises above the machinations of the censor to stick to her own truth. She becomes a beacon. And again, "The censors can't stand light."

Choose two of the four types of manipulation used by censors that are discussed above. For each, list all the evidences of it found in the novel. Include the evidences already mentioned.

Name: _____ Date: _____

Names

"Even though he did make mistakes, Mr. O'Malley was a lot of fun."

Barney's mother had a very clear reason for naming him as she did. His name had great significance for her, both emotionally and intellectually. The name embodied a beautiful idea. She hoped her child, like Mr. O'Malley, would know what it was like to be wonderful, magical, and fun, *as well as* free to make mistakes.

Deirdre's name also has significance. She knows the story of its history very well, and despite the beauty of the name, she seems to feel a sadness about it. Of course, the story itself is one of great sadness.

What about your name? Who named you? Why was your name chosen? Do you have a middle name? What is its significance? Do you know the history and meaning of your last name? Do you have a nickname? What does it mean?

On the paper below, brainstorm everything you know about your name. Talk to your parents or anyone else who may know something about the significance of your name. Look in baby-naming books for the meaning of your name. If your last name is fairly common, it will be relatively easy to research its meaning. If you cannot locate a dependable authority, take your best guess as to the meaning.

When you are finished, choose one item about your name to share with the class. After all, names are often part of who we are.

My Name

_____   _____

_____   _____

_____   _____

_____   _____

_____   _____

_____   _____

_____   _____

Name: _____ Date: _____

What Do You Think?

In a celebration of free thinking, list your first response to each of the following.

1. What is your favorite color?

    _____

2. What is your favorite place?

    _____

3. What is your favorite thing to wear?

    _____

4. What is your favorite name?

    _____

5. Whom do you most admire?

    _____

6. What is your favorite thing to do?

    _____

7. Where would you like to go on vacation?

    _____

8. What is your favorite song?

    _____

9. What is your favorite book?

    _____

10. What is your favorite food?

    _____

11. What is your favorite sport to play?

    _____

12. What are your favorite qualities about yourself?

    _____

13. Name one thing that is attractive about you.

    _____

14. Name one thing that is special about you.

    _____

15. Name one thing in which you really believe.

    _____

Share some of these things with the class if you choose.

Physical Freedom

The Limitless Opportunity to Move

Name: _____ Date: _____

Where Would You Like to Go?

Take a look at the map below. Imagine you have an entire day to travel around anywhere you would like. You can go inside houses and buildings, through parks and backyards, down below the city in the sewer system—anywhere! There are no limits to your ability to wander around and investigate. On the back of this paper, write where you will go.

FREEDOM TOWN

Name: _____ Date: _____

Motion Wordsearch

All of the words in the wordsearch below have to do with motion. Can you find them all?

```
Q R I M P E L D P E K A O D N E L L N E
M N S K T K T H G I L F P Q J K O S Q S
O B H O V E R L D R A N V Y E M C L T W
T A Q I G H A N R H W K C R I I O N L A
I B U D G E N S P G B M X C T H M W R N
V D B K L F S P E E D O V E H D O D G D
A W E D I P I A M O R B N H N B T L Y E
T W F N D A T K D B R I K E L D I N U R
E J L T E S L C D J K L V D K Y O P L U
D T O A M S M S M O B I L I T Y N G J K
U N W M W K C K K U V Z H L E V A R T H
B E Y J V I S D F R L E M S P L S R T U
R M O T I O N B D N L J U R E V O M T E
K E J S T Z Y T C E M L J P P E W D F G
L V B G T E U A M Y S W O K S R E L G D
F O F W H I T Y G L D R I F T S I X O O
G M A W L V R F Q E P E B F H T R L B D
```

Word Bank

budge	impel	move	stir
dodge	journey	movement	transit
drift	kinetic	pass	travel
flight	locomotion	propel	voyage
flit	mobility	ran	walk
flow	mobilize	run	wander
glide	motion	slide	
hover	motivate	speed	

Name: _____ Date: _____

Slavery

Slavery began in the United States in the 1600's. It was most prominent in the South, for it was there that large plantations dominated. They required many workers to maintain operations, and the relatively free labor the slaves provided was more profitable than hired labor. The North's economy depended more particularly on industry and small farms; therefore, the perceived need for slaves was less.

From the Revolutionary War throughout the 1800's, slavery became increasingly controversial. Prominent leaders spoke out against the human injustice and immorality. Others justified slavery with rationalizations that supported the underlying tug of economics. Perhaps the greatest pull against slavery was the revolution itself, for many people saw the hypocrisy of a nation founded on individual freedom where millions of people had virtually none.

Not only were slaves owned, as the term *slave* indicates, but they were usually kept in the basest of conditions. Countless narratives direct from slaves themselves tell of one-room cabins where a dozen people may live, sleeping on the dirt floor, wearing only the coarsest of clothes and shoes, if shoes were available at all. Slaves could not legally marry, had no rights to their own children, and usually could not acquire any education. They certainly could not own any property and, most definitely, they had no say in government. Slaves were not allowed to gather together in any numbers without the consent of their masters. Field hands usually worked from sunup to sundown. House servants worked perhaps fewer hours but were at the constant bidding of their masters. Punishments were often harsh and inhumane. No wonder that uprisings and abolitionists were on the rise.

Try to imagine yourself in the life of a slave. You are not free to leave; you must do as you are told. You are ruled through fear. How do you feel? Imagine what one of your days is like. Write a description below and on the back of this paper of your day and your feelings from your imagined perspective as a slave.

When finished, share with the class some actual narratives from individuals who lived that life. Two good resources for such narratives are Julius Lester's *To Be a Slave* (Dial, 1968) and Paul D. Escott's *Slavery Remembered: A Record of Twentieth-Century Slave Narratives* (University of North Carolina Press, 1979).

Slave Days   Date:

Name: _____ Date: _____

The Proslavery Movement

As the voices of abolitionists grew louder and stronger in the United States in the 1800's, a new movement sprang up in the southern states. It was called the Proslavery Movement. Proponents of this movement declared that nature itself supported slavery because in nature the strong always rule the weak. They also asserted that the Bible supports their system, and that, in fact, black slaves were better off under slavery, for they had security, food, shelter, clothing, and living conditions better than those of Africa. They also declared fervently that the entire economy of the South would collapse without slave labor.

These viewpoints are appalling for some obvious reasons, perhaps even more so because they were ardently believed. Rebut the arguments of the Proslavery Movement here.

Proslavery Movement Rebuttal

1. How are the arguments flawed?

   _____

   _____

   _____

   _____

   _____

2. What basic truths are denied?

   _____

   _____

   _____

   _____

   _____

3. What other arguments are there against slavery?

   _____

   _____

   _____

   _____

   _____

Name: _____ Date: _____

Travel Equations

Freedom to move sometimes requires intellectual activity as well. Plans and projections for all sorts of things need to be considered before setting out. Work out the following problems to illustrate how some careful thought oftentimes works hand-in-hand with movement. (Note: Approximate your answers to the nearest mile or quarter hour.)

1. You have 10 gallons (38 L) of gas in your car. Your car travels at 33 miles per gallon (13.9 km/L) on the open highway. How many miles (km) can you travel on this tank of gas?

2. Look on a map to determine the farthest town you could reach from your hometown right now on the above tank of gas. What town is it? How many miles (km) are there between your town and the town to which you can travel?

3. You are travelling from Portland, Oregon, to Cheyenne, Wyoming. The distance is 1,206 miles (1929.6 km). You've stopped in Boise, Idaho, and you have 762 miles (1219.2 km) to go. How far have you travelled already?

4. Using the locations and distances in problem three, how many miles (km) would you need to travel each day in order to divide your remaining trip evenly into three days?

5. If you drove 60 miles (96 km) per hour each day, how many hours each day would you need to drive in order to travel the number of miles (km) determined in problem four above?

6. Plane travel from San Francisco, California, to Los Angeles, California, is 45 minutes. The distance is approximately 410 miles (656 km). Driving 55 miles (88 km) per hour, how much longer would travel by car take than travel by plane?

7. San Diego, California, is approximately 120 miles (192 km) south of Los Angeles. If you flew from San Francisco to L.A., then drove from L.A. to San Diego at 55 miles (88km) per hour, how much travel time would you need?

8. Buffalo, New York, is approximately 1,700 miles (2720 km) from Amarillo, Texas. Amarillo is approximately 1,700 miles (2720 km) from Seattle, Washington. Seattle is approximately 2,700 miles (4320 km) from Buffalo. What is the area between the three locations? (Note: Area for a triangle is ½ (base x height). To get the height for this isosceles triangle, you will have to use the Pythagorean Theorem. If you do not know it, it can be found in the encyclopedia.)

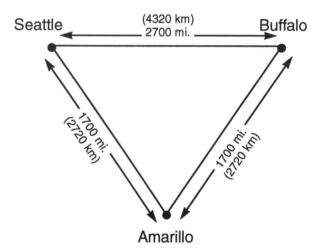

9. If planes travelled at 400 miles (640 km) per hour, how long would each of the above three trips take?

10. If Grand Island, Nebraska, were right in the middle of the triangle formed by the three locations above, do you have enough information to determine how many miles (km) away it is from each?

Chess

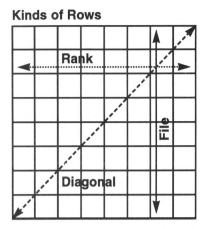

The game of chess is all about movement. Some pieces (called *men*) on the chessboard are more powerful than others, but each has some restrictions as to movement.

Follow the illustrations to make individual chessboards. Rows running across are called *rank*. Rows running up and down are called *file*. Rows at an angle are called *diagonals*. On a chessboard, each of the two players has at his/her right-hand corner a light-colored square.

The men on a chessboard are either dark in color or light; the dark colored pieces are called *black* and the light colored ones are called *white*. Each set consists of one *king*, one *queen*, two *rooks*, two *bishops*, two *knights*, and eight *pawns*. The object of each team is to trap the opposing team's king while protecting its own. A man can capture any man of the opposing team by moving to its square and replacing it there. Each student can make men out of dark and light paper, writing the name of each man on it.

Chess is a complicated game, full of strategy and, upon occasion, exceptions to the rules.

All of these rules can be acquired with the purchase of a chessboard, or more simply, in an encyclopedia. For now, basic movements on the chessboard can be practiced.

Arrange the players according to illustration A. See illustrations B and C for their allowable movements. The king can move in all directions, one space at a time. The queen can move in all directions in any number of squares. The rooks may move in rank or file, any number of squares. The bishops may move diagonally, any number of squares. The knights may move in an L-shape, one rank up or down and two files left or right, or vice versa. The pawn can move one or two squares forward on its first move, but only one square at a time after that. The pawn captures by moving at a diagonal next to the piece being captured.

Have students practice moving the pieces until they remember easily how each is allowed to move. Now have students challenge one another in small groups, as a class, or individually by making up situations on a chessboard and analyzing which move is best to make.

B. The king may move in any direction but only one square at a time. The queen may move any number of squares in any direction. The rook may move on any rank or file any number of squares.

C. The bishop may move any number of squares but only diagonally. The knight makes L-shaped moves as shown. The pawn may travel either one or two squares on its first move, but only one square at a time after that. It captures other pieces by moving diagonally.

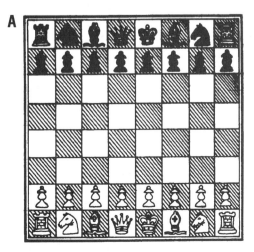

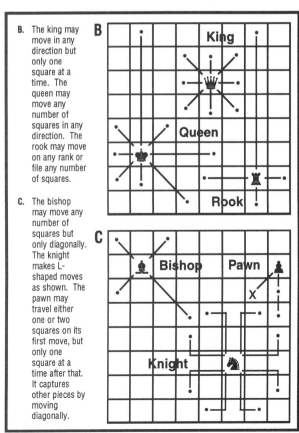

Physical Challenge Awareness Day

Some restraints on physical freedom do not come from the outside world but are due, instead, to personal physical challenges. One way to bring about an empathetic sensitivity to such challenges is to have a day of awareness in your class or school. Volunteers can choose a method by which to restrict themselves physically for a day. For example, a student might choose to wear a blindfold or ear plugs, walk on crutches, or move about in a wheelchair for the duration of one day. At the close of the day, participants can gather to discuss their feelings about their experiences of the day. They might also have something to say about the school's sensitivity to physical challenges in the way of ramps and wheelchair-accessible restrooms, for example.

Use the form below to take pledges to participate in the Physical Challenge Awareness Day.

Physical Challenge Awareness Day

I, _____ ,

pledge to participate in

PHYSICAL CHALLENGE AWARENESS DAY,

to be held in my class/school on _____ .

For the day, I choose to live with the physical challenge of

_____ .

I understand that at the end of the day, all participants will gather to discuss

our feelings and reactions to our experiences.

Together we can bring about greater awareness of the needs of

physically challenged people.

Name: _____ Date: _____

Personal Effects of Slavery

There are conditions common to the existence of a slave. She works long hours without compensation. He has no free time with which to follow his own pursuits. She is not allowed to marry, nor does she have the guarantee that she will be allowed to stay with and raise her children. His natural tendency to gain and build friendships is, at the least, unsupported and, at the most, prohibited. Her need for education is kept without satisfaction. His desire to have and make a home is nullified, for his home belongs to his master. Her right to her own body to use and protect as she wishes is removed. Please note, each of the above conditions may be understood to apply to both men and women. Neither has any of these normal and natural freedoms.

What, then, can you surmise are the physical and emotional effects of slavery on an individual? Given that everything listed in the paragraph above is understood in democratic civilizations to be the natural right and instinct of every individual, what effects does the removal of these freedoms have on that individual? Think about everything from quality of life to life expectancy.

What do you guess are the normal physical and emotional outcomes of a life lived under slavery?

Brainstorm your ideas here. Then share them in the class and discuss.

Extension:

As a follow-up, look into slave narratives or any essays and research you can find on this issue. What do they say?

Interactive Art

The artist Jackson Pollock liked to place his canvas on the floor. He felt that in this way he could interact physically with the art, even becoming part of it in a kinetic-emotional way. Pollock is perhaps best known for his many works in which, placing the canvas on the floor, he dropped, splattered, and sprinkled paint of various colors in patterns and visual rhythms meant to convey moods and feelings. For Pollock, this method also helped him to "become" part of his work.

Part of the modern movement of art in all forms is the interaction of the artist with his/her art. This can be done on an emotional level, as is always the case with creativity, or on a literal level through the actual use of the artist's body in the work. Young children do this all the time when they fingerpaint or make fingerprint art. Some people even go so far as to permanently mix art and their bodies by having tattoos imprinted on themselves. Women and men alike use make-up to "paint" themselves. Even clothing and hair styles are an artistic expression.

Create your own "body" work by using parts of your body—hands, feet, elbows, knees—together with paint and a large sheet of paper and canvas. This project will definitely be messy, so be sure to wear old clothes and use water-soluble paint. You can even do an interactive painting with yourself and a friend or two. The whole class can do a giant fingerpainting!

If you feel inhibited, take any opportunity you have (even a field trip to a local preschool) to watch children fingerpaint. They know how to enjoy what they are doing without limiting themselves for fear of what others will think or of getting messy. (The messier the better, they say!) The little kid inside you probably knows how, too. So let that little kid have a ball!

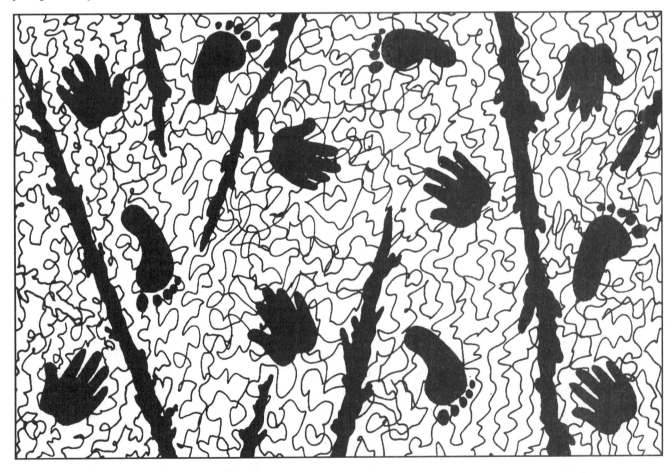

Hands-On Freedom Activities

Murals

As a class, paint a giant mural on butcher paper or a wall (if you get permission) depicting any symbols and scenes of physical freedom that you can think of. Be sure to plan your mural ahead of time and block it out to use your space well. Some symbols and scenes that you might use are broken chains and fences, arms raised in freedom, the "Emancipation Proclamation," the Underground Railroad, and so forth.

Paper Chains

Make a giant paper chain by gluing circles of drab colored paper through each other. String this giant chain around the walls of your classroom, breaking it at a bulletin board. On the bulletin board, spell out in brightly colored letters ". . . and the chains shall be broken." You may use another phrase if you like. Each student can then affix a paper naming a freedom that he or she enjoys.

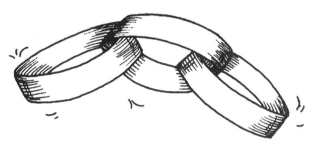

Daisy Chains

Daisy chains are made by cutting small slits near the top of a daisy stem, then inserting the stem of another daisy through this. Slit the stem of the second daisy, and so on. Stems can be woven in a circle to make a wreath.

You can also make flower chains out of colored paper. Simply make flowers and stems, slitting the stems as above. Either way, you can discuss the beauty of this kind of chain and the brutality of the other when they are used to restrict people in slavery.

Collage

Students can cut pictures and words from magazines and newspapers and collage them together in honor of physical freedom. They can even collage them in the shape of a symbol that represents freedom, such as a dove or the Statue of Liberty. The whole class can work on a giant-sized collage, small groups can make them, or individuals can make their own.

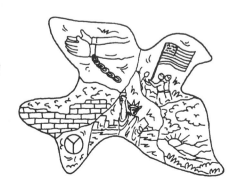

Music and Dance

Martha Graham was a dancer and choreographer who broke the traditional boundaries of dance. She felt that dance was meant to expose "the inner landscape," or the feelings that each of us carries inside. In both the motive behind her dance and her style of dance, she was a real pioneer, always at the forefront of the modern dance movement.

Graham lived for almost 100 years, dancing until the end. She lived the idea that the biggest limitations on the human body are the ones we impose ourselves.

The movements which Martha Graham choreographed were sometimes sharp and abrupt, angular and jerky. This was not the typical graceful and fluid motion of a ballerina. Graham broke that tradition by showing that there was something more, something equally beautiful, though perhaps disturbing instead of serene.

Always, music was integral to Graham's dance. The music, too, reflected the mood. As a class, choose two or three pieces of instrumental music. Make sure that each reflects a different feeling. (Vivaldi's *Four Seasons* may be a good choice, because each concerto evokes the feelings of that season. Also good would be a blues or other jazz selection, and a rock instrumental, because the feelings of each are likely to be distinct.) Play each piece of music and close your eyes. Play each piece a second time, this time individually choosing a body movement that reflects the emotion of the music. Put the motions chosen by each member of the class together to make a dance. Everyone can learn the dance in its entirety.

Name: _____ Date: _____

Spirituals

Black spirituals grew out of slavery. For many, the only hope for freedom was in life after death. The words of spirituals combined the beliefs of traditional African religions and music with Christianity. Of particular interest was the Judeo-Christian story of the Israelites who, led by Moses, gained freedom from bondage. Spirituals were also popular because they could be sung together while working, thus creating something of a spirit of community. Finally, it is said that some spirituals had hidden within them secret messages about a tangible way to freedom—namely, the Underground Railroad.

For whatever reason, spirituals have endured to the present time. For many people, spirituals are beloved not only for their rhythms and musical beauty, but because they carry within them great hope for freedom and a strong sense of faith in the eventual order of things.

Below are the words to two famous spirituals. One of these and other spirituals worth note can be found in the wonderful book, *All Night, All Day: A Child's First Book of African-American Spirituals,* edited and illustrated by Ashley Bryan (Atheneum, 1991). Read the spirituals given here and write on the back of this page what each means to you.

Swing Low, Sweet Chariot

Swing low, sweet chariot,
Coming for to carry me home.
Swing low, sweet chariot,
Coming for to carry me home.

I looked over Jordan, and what did I see,
Coming for to carry me home?
A band of angels coming after me,
Coming for to carry me home.

Swing low, sweet chariot,
Coming for to carry me home.
Swing low, sweet chariot,
Coming for to carry me home.

He's Got the Whole World in His Hands

He's got the whole world in his hands,
He's got the whole world in his hands,
He's got the whole world in his hands,
He's got the whole world in his hands.

He's got the wind and the rain in his hands,
He's got the wind and the rain in his hands,
He's got the wind and the rain in his hands,
He's got the whole world in his hands.

He's got the little bitty baby in his hands,
He's got the little bitty baby in his hands,
He's got the little bitty baby in his hands,
He's got the whole world in his hands.

He's got you and me, brother, in his hands,
He's got you and me, sister, in his hands,
He's got you and me, brother, in his hands,
He's got the whole world in his hands.

Recipe for Hardtack

Throughout history, there is record of travellers on long journeys carrying with them types of unleavened bread. From the Israelites fleeing Egypt to Civil War soldiers carrying their own rations, hardtack of one sort or another has been a staple. Here is one recipe.

Hardtack

Ingredients and Materials:

- 3 cups (750 mL) all-purpose flour
- additional flour for kneading
- 3 teaspoons (15 mL) salt
- 1 cup (250 mL) water
- rolling pin
- baking sheet
- bowl
- nail

Directions:

1. Mix the flour and salt in the bowl.

2. Add the water, mixing as long as you can.

3. Knead the dough, adding flour as you knead to make the dough very dry.

4. Roll the dough into a rectangle, using your hands to help as needed. Roll to $\frac{1}{2}$ (1.25 cm) inch thick.

5. Cut into 3-inch (8 cm) squares.

6. Punch 12–16 holes in each square with the tip of a clean or sterilized nail. (The nail holes will make the hardtack easier to break apart.)

7. Place the squares on the baking sheet and bake for 30 minutes. The hardtack will be light brown and crisp like a cracker.

8. To eat the hardtack easily after it has cooled, it must be soaked in water. Otherwise, it is too hard to be edible.

Name: _____ Date: _____

What I Need for Survival

A common sight in a television situation-comedy of the fifties or sixties was a young child running away from home with a stick flung over his/her shoulder and a knapsack tied to the end of the stick. Anything might have been in that sack, from peanut-butter-and-jelly sandwiches to a favorite pet frog. A young child would not necessarily think of necessities for survival but rather necessities for comfort.

What about you? If you were to survive on your own, what things would you absolutely need for physical survival? Also, what things would you want for your added comfort and pleasure?

In the columns below, brainstorm the things which are necessities and the things which you would like. Then share them with the class. Make a class chart of necessities and likes. Are any of the "necessities" really not necessary?

Survival

What I Need	What I Would Like

Challenge for Discussion:

If people have their basic needs met, is that enough for their survival and well-being?

Traditional Games About Breaking Free

Red Rover

There is a traditional children's game that perfectly simulates the experience of physical restriction and breaking free. It is *Red Rover.* If you do not already know how to play, follow these simple directions.

Two teams are chosen, each team having an equal number of players (from 3 upwards to anything). During play, each team joins hands in a long line, facing the opposing team. Keep at least a dozen feet (preferably more) between the two teams.

Flip a coin or have a team representative chose a number to see which team goes first. That team consults together to agree upon one member of the opposing team to call over. Then they hold hands and swing their arms, chanting:

"Red Rover, Red Rover, send (name of person selected) right over."

The person who has been called breaks hands with his/her team and runs toward the other team. He/she tries to break through the grip of any two members of the opposing team. If he/she succeeds, the runner may return to his/her group. If he/she can't break through, the runner becomes a member of the opposing team and joins hands with them.

It is now the turn of the opposing team to agree upon a member from the first team and then call him/her over using the chant. Play continues in this way until one team is left with only one player.

Variation: When a runner breaks through the line of the opposing team, that runner may bring a member of the opposing team back with him/her.

Hide and Seek

Though there may be few who do not know how this game is played, here are some directions to refresh everyone's memory. As is the case with any popular, traditional game, certain directions may vary according to regional area. Everyone is free to offer the rules and directions he/she remembers.

At least two players are needed. The number can expand to as many as desired. A tree or other marker is chosen as "home." One player is chosen as "It." It stands at home and closes his/her eyes. It then counts to 20 while the others hide within a previously designated area. When It has finished counting, he/she hollers, "Ready or not, here I come," and begins searching for the others. When It spies one, he/she shouts, "I spy (name of person spied)," and runs home. The spied player also runs home. If the spied player tags home first, he/she shouts, "Free!" If It tags home first, he/she shouts, "Ollie-ollie-oxen-free!" (All the, all the outs in free!) This shows that It has caught another player and that all other players can come out of hiding. The tagged player then becomes It, and It joins the others to hide again.

Variation: Any player may come out of hiding while It is searching. He/she then runs for home to shout, "Free!" hoping that It will not see him/her until that player is safely home. Other variations may occur in this game, from one region to another.

The Underground Railroad

At the bottom of this page, you will find one way to simulate the Underground Railroad. Students are free and welcome to imagine and plan other ways as well.

The Underground Railroad was developed as an escape system for runaway slaves during the times of legal slavery in the United States. Harriet Tubman is perhaps the best known "conductor" of the Underground Railroad. She helped countless slaves escape from the South to freedom in the North.

The Underground Railroad was not an actual railway line, but a discreet route of houses and rest stations where runaways could stop for food, shelter, and directions to the next safe stop. Runaway slaves had a great deal to risk. If caught, not only would they be returned to slavery, but they would likely be severely punished as well. There are stories of individuals whose attempts at running away failed, and their punishment was the loss or maiming of a foot to make such running impossible. In order to reach freedom, the slaves needed to trust absolute strangers, and that alone was an enormous risk. The individuals helping the slaves, both free blacks and whites, were also at risk of being caught and punished themselves. However, they knew that the freedom of every individual was worth their personal risk. Travel was almost always on foot. Conditions were harsh, but the hope for freedom on the other end was enough to make both the trip and the challenge worthwhile for many.

Simulation

To simulate your own Underground Railroad, divide into three teams. The first team will represent the slaves who are seeking freedom. The second team will represent the conductors of the Underground Railroad. The third team will represent the slave masters and law enforcers. Each team should have an opportunity to represent each group; therefore, three full rounds of "play" are necessary.

For each cycle, the Underground Railroad team will need to meet to plan an escape route. The teacher should be given a written copy of that route. The law enforcement team will also meet to plan their posts. They will give a copy of their posts to the teacher, as well. Each member of the Underground Railroad will take up a post (some posts can be decoys). The first member along the route will begin the "slaves" on their way to freedom, either one at a time, in small groups, or all at once. The last player of the Underground Railroad team will represent the North. When play begins, all players of the law enforcement team will stand at the posts they have pre-determined. A slave has been captured when he/she is seen and tagged by a member of the law-enforcement team.

This may work best as an after-school activity or in some area of the school where others will not be disturbed. Play can be altered as the class wishes.

When play is complete, discuss as a class how it felt to be a member of each group.

The Slave Dancer

by Paula Fox (Dell, 1973)

(Available in Canada, Dell; UK, Macmillan Educ.; Australia, Transworld Publishers)

Summary: The year is 1840, and the location is New Orleans' French Quarter. While his mother works at home as a seamstress to the rich and his younger sister plays cat's cradle and other childhood games, thirteen-year-old Jessie Bollier wanders through the market and trading places of the city, playing his pipe now and then for the pennies he might earn. One fateful day he does earn a small sum from sailors along the wharf. He regrets this later when, sent by his mother to borrow some candles from his hard-hearted Aunt Agatha, Jessie is abducted in a back alley by the sailors for whom he played earlier. Though he then falls unconscious, he wakes later on a raft bound for the sailors' ship, the *Moonlight*. Jessie learns that he has been kidnapped and that the sailors intend for him to take their next voyage with them. Moreover, he is to use his pipe to play for the ship's cargo: slaves.

On board the ship, Jessie meets its foreboding crew. Ben Stout is the first to befriend him, but Jessie soon becomes aware that there is something untrustworthy, and even sinister, in Stout. Though harsh, Purvis, one of his abductors, is a truer friend to Jessie than is Ben, and Jessie grows quite fond of him. Captain Cawthorne is another case altogether. The man seems virtually insane as, upon meeting Jessie, he grabs him up and bites his ear until it bleeds. Nine more sailors of various temperaments and personalities round out the crew, and together they set sail across the Atlantic to the shores of Africa.

During the trip, Jessie learns the ways of ships and sailors. Like the others, he is made to work during all waking hours. Still, the trip is bearable until they reach Africa and the slaves come aboard. Jessie is appalled and grieved by the treatment of other human beings in so careless and degrading a manner. He tries to show his outrage and fight the actions of Cawthorne and the crew; however, he soon learns that to defend the rights of the slaves is to take on the wrath and scorn of his shipmates. They have each justified their actions for themselves to such an extent that they even believe their cause somehow right and just.

Soon after the slaves arrive, Jessie learns the purpose of his pipe. In the mornings, he is to "dance" the slaves for their exercise. He plays while they shuffle their feet and move as best they can while in shackles and near starvation. Jessie is sickened by the whole business, yet he, too, is a captive and has no recourse.

As the trip wears on, slaves and crew alike begin to die for reasons of illness, hunger, and physical torment. At last, on the eve of the slaves being sold in Cuba, law enforcement ships approach the *Moonlight,* and in a panic the slaves are thrown overboard to the shark-infested waters. This horrendous action is followed directly by a terrible storm at sea in which the entire crew perishes and the ship goes down. However, there are two survivors, Jessie and one young black boy, Ras. The two somehow swim to shore. An old black man named Daniel, living a hidden life in the woods of Mississippi to preserve his freedom, finds them on the sand. He takes care of them for several weeks, and then arranges for Ras to be secreted to the North where he will be free. He gives Jessie provisions and directions to walk his way home to Louisiana. Jessie does and meets there in joyful reunion with his mother and sister. Slowly his life is restored to normal. Yet, there is one thing Jessie has lost. He can never again bear to hear music played of any kind. The memories are too vivid and the feelings too intense.

Name: _____ Date: _____

The Characters

Following is a partial list of characters from *The Slave Dancer* by Paula Fox. Next to each, write down one thing that Jessie says about him/her that lets you, the reader, know something about that character.

1. Jessie Bollier _____

2. Aunt Agatha _____

3. Purvis _____

4. Claudius Sharkey _____

5. Benjamin Stout _____

6. Nick Spark _____

7. Captain Cawthorne _____

8. Cook (Curry) _____

9. Ned Grime _____

10. Ras _____

11. Daniel_____

From the novel, it is clear that each character is "trapped" in some way, either literally or figuratively. Choose any four characters from the above list and write how each is trapped.

1. _____ is "trapped" in this way: _____

    _____

    _____

2. _____ is "trapped" in this way: _____

    _____

    _____

3. _____ is "trapped" in this way: _____

    _____

    _____

4. _____ is "trapped" in this way: _____

    _____

    _____

Name: _____ Date: _____

New Orleans

Below is a map of New Orleans. Using the novel as a guide, respond to the following questions:

1. Approximately where do you think Jessie's home is located? _____

   _____

2. In what direction is he taken when abducted? _____

   _____

3. Why do you think New Orleans has always been such an excellent location for trade? _____

   _____

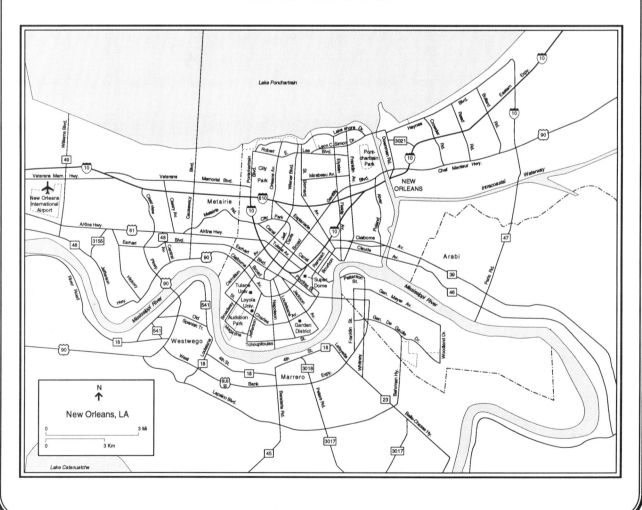

Sewing

Until 1846, most sewing was done by hand. In that year, Elias Howe patented the first practical sewing machine. More than anything, it freed people who had been bogged down in the painstaking work of stitching long and even seams, strong bindings, and countless firm buttonholes.

The simplest hand stitch is the running stitch. It is made by bringing the threaded needle up through the fabric and then down again a short distance forward. The step is repeated until the entire seam is sewn. Yet, even the running stitch, simple as it is, requires care, patience, and precision when done by hand. The most particular seamstresses required almost impossible numbers of even stitches within a one-inch (2.5 cm) length.

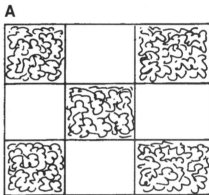

A

To illustrate the skill needed to sew, try making one square for a patchwork quilt. Using the pattern below, cut out nine squares of equal size. Use as many different fabrics as you wish. For example, you may want every square to be different, or you may want the fabrics to alternate in a checkerboard fashion. (See illustration A.) On a flat surface, arrange your nine squares in front of you in any desired patchwork pattern.

Use chalk on the reverse side of each square to mark a 1/4" (.6 cm) seam all around the edge. (See illustration B.) Hold together two squares that go next to each other in the patchwork design, right sides facing in. (See illustration C.) Stitch these two pieces together on the chalk line. Continue this process by sewing on each piece in its correct order. When you have sewn on all pieces (if you have been careful and precise), you will have a perfect patchwork square.

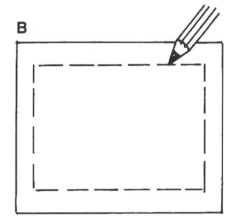

B

Note: All the patchwork squares made by the class members can be sewn together to make a full-size patchwork quilt.

Square Pattern

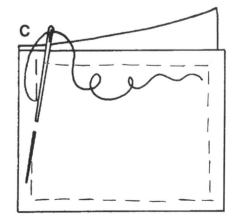

C

Name: _____ Date: _____

Clippers

Clippers got their name because of their speed. They were said to "clip off" the miles due to their slender hulls and multiple sails. They were designed to make the long trip from the United States to China for purposes of trade. In the novel *The Slave Dancer,* a clipper is also used for trade, but this time speed is required for reasons other than monetary.

Clippers were built and used in the mid-1800's, so they would have been relatively modern ships at the time of the novel. They gained instant popularity. The reasons may seem obvious.

In your own words, how do you think that the invention of the clipper affected the freedom of . . .

1. Merchants?_____

    _____

2. Pirates?_____

    _____

3. Naval forces? _____

    _____

4. Travellers? _____

    _____

Name: _____ Date: _____

Pipes and Panic

The ancient Greek god of the woods and pastures is known as Pan. His form is half man and half goat. He is said to be wild and unpredictable, a rogue, and a source of terror in almost anyone who crosses his path. Yet, this same Pan, paradoxically, is perhaps best known for the beautiful harmonies which he draws from his pipe made of reed.

Pan acquired his pipe in this way. In one of his many pursuits of nymphs and deities, he tried to begin an affair with one named Syrinx. However, Syrinx wanted nothing from the strange and mischievous Pan, so she ran in fear to the gods. To protect her, they changed her into a bed of reeds. Pan discovered the reeds, and from one he made a pipe, or panpipe.

Besides being credited as the originator of the musical pipe, Pan is also to be thanked for one word in the English language: *panic.* It is this response that everyone has when meeting him.

Feelings such as panic have a great effect on the body. Syrinx ran in her terror. Various emotions may also make our hearts race, our mouths dry up, our hands shake, or our bodies shiver. What happens to you, physically, when you experience each of the following emotions?

1. Fear _____

   _____

2. Sadness _____

   _____

3. Joy _____

   _____

4. Anger _____

   _____

5. Embarrassment _____

   _____

6. Panic _____

   _____

Name: _____ Date: _____

Pirates and Flags

The presence and practices of pirates throughout time have certainly affected the freedoms of other travellers, even if those travellers do not have the purest of intentions in their own missions (like the crew of the *Moonlight*). Pirates have existed as long as there have been ships on which they could sail. Individuals have always had many reasons for turning to piracy. Sometimes honest and hardworking seamen have become pirates after mutinying against the harsh conditions of their sea life. Some have sought out the adventure and wealth that piracy can bring. Still others have turned to piracy after wars have ended and they are no longer needed as privateers. (Privateers are employed by governments during wartime to raid and loot the enemy on the seas.)

Life for a pirate was usually not a happy one. Sea conditions were most often miserable, and other pirates were certainly not to be trusted. The work was hard and unceasing. Though it is strange to say, pirates often ran a tight ship. As is the case in *The Slave Dancer,* seamen of any kind can never afford to be lax in the upkeep of their ship. Their very lives depend upon it.

Pirate ships, like all other sailing vessels, often flew a flag to let others know their affiliation. On the *Moonlight,* the flags are changed according to the needs of the current situation. Pirates would have little need to hide their identity unless they feared being overtaken. Usually, however, they were doing the overtaking. Some of the most nefarious pirates of all time were identifiable through the flags they flew. Most people are familiar with the *Jolly Roger* (the traditional skull and crossbones), a universal flag of piracy flown by any number of pirates. But given below are three other flags that belonged to specific pirates. Just as another ship could easily identify the flag of the United States, Spain, or Great Britain, so too could they identify the flags of these infamous pirates.

Emanuel Wynne	Bartholomew Roberts	Edward Low
	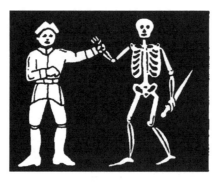	

Many would argue that the *Moonlight* is also a pirate ship, marauding and invading the homes and lives of innocent people. If the *Moonlight* had a pirate flag of its own, what do you think it would be? Draw your design on the back.

Name: _____ Date: _____

Colors

In *The Slave Dancer,* Jessie twice mentions something because of its vibrant colors. The first time, he describes the beautiful basket of silken threads in the otherwise dreary apartment. The second time, he describes a glorious flying fish he spies from his workplace on board the *Moonlight.* Each thing symbolizes for him something better than what he is currently experiencing, perhaps a hope for a world of color beyond his bleak surroundings.

Color usually does illustrate a world of life and joy and wonder. Just as Dorothy opens the door to color in the movie *The Wizard of Oz,* Jessie is ready to open the door and let in all the rainbows the world has to offer.

Below, draw and color a flying fish or basket of threads in the most vibrant and beautiful colors you can. Explain below it or on the back how this thing can symbolize freedom for Jessie.

Colors for Freedom

Africa

Below is a map of Africa. Find the Bight of Benin. Mark the approximate location of the *Moonlight*.

Looking at the map, can you guess the likely homelands of the people sold to Captain Cawthorne? In an encyclopedia, research one of those countries. Take notes about that country's history of selling its people into slavery as well as the abduction of people from that country by natives of other countries. Report your findings to the class.

Africa

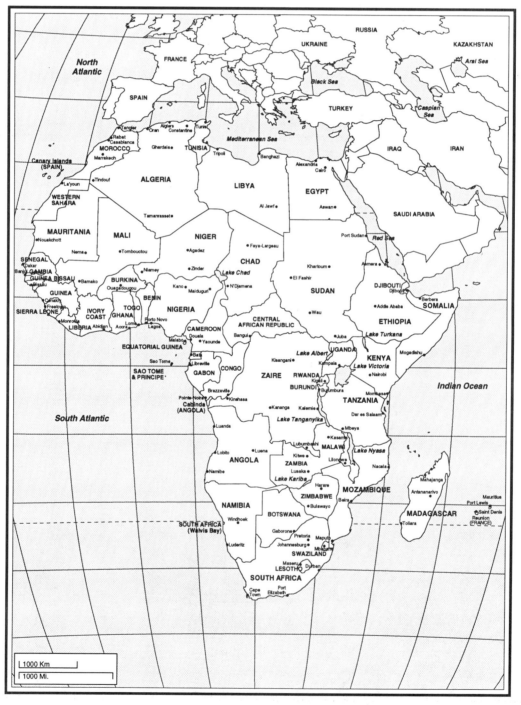

Name: _____ Date: _____

What Would They Say?

If one of the characters on board the *Moonlight* kept a journal about his/her feelings and experiences, those feelings would likely be intense and those experiences harrowing. Taking on the persona of any character you choose, write your account of and reaction to any day aboard the *Moonlight*. Use the journal page below, and be sure to sign the character's name at the bottom. (If the character's name is not given, you can write a brief identification of that character at the bottom of the page.)

One Day Aboard the *Moonlight*

Signed _____

Journey to Topaz

by Yoshiko Uchida (Creative Arts Book Company, 1971)

(Availability outside U.S.—510-848-4777)

Summary: It is December of 1941, and eleven-year-old Yuki Sakane is excited about the upcoming holidays. Hers is the happy life of a young adolescent, growing up in the love and security of a close-knit family. Her older brother, Kenichi, is a student at the nearby University of California at Berkeley. Her father is a prominent and well-respected businessman of Japanese birth, revered for his gentleness and peacemaking abilities. Her mother is a homemaker who takes great joy in providing comfort and pleasure for her family and friends. Both Mr. and Mrs. Sakane have lived in the United States for twenty years, though law has forbidden them to become citizens. But the lives and pleasures of all change drastically with a simple knock at the door one December day. Standing there are agents of the U.S. Federal Bureau of Investigation.

On December 7, 1941, the country of Japan bombs Pearl Harbor in the United States, and the life of Yuki Sakane is turned upside-down. She and thousands of other Japanese Americans living on the West Coast of the U.S. are labelled "enemy aliens," and their freedoms are gradually taken away. First, Mr. Sakane is called in for questioning by the F.B.I. agents. He is not allowed to return home, but instead is taken with other prominent leaders of Japanese descent to a prison camp in Montana. After a few months, the families of these men, in fact all Japanese (even those who are full citizens of the United States) living on the West Coast, are evacuated to temporary concentration camps near their home. They must sell, store, or give away nearly all their belongings. They are allowed to take with them only what they can carry. Anything that might be used against the United States, from cameras to binoculars, is confiscated by the government as contraband. Then, after four months in the temporary camp, Yuki, her mother, and her brother are taken to a permanent camp in Topaz, Utah.

Conditions there are harsh and depressing, but the resilient spirit of Yuki keeps her thriving and interested in life. Others, like Ken, become more and more depressed over their confinement. Yuki makes friends with others in the camp and looks for the good to enjoy in life. Ken has his friends, but he becomes more and more withdrawn. Though it is possible for him to leave camp by going to a university in the East or Midwest, he feels an obligation to his mother and sister in his father's absence.

Finally, after a full year passes and it is December again, Mr. Sakane is released on parole and is able to return to his family. His son, Ken, also makes a move, this time not to a university but to join with the U.S. army as a soldier fighting in World War II. He wishes to prove his loyalty as a citizen of the U.S., despite its illegal actions of interning its people regardless of their rights under the Constitution.

Finally, the three remaining family members are released when Mr. Sakane acquires a permit to seek employment in nearby Salt Lake City, Utah. They are still not permitted to return to the West, but they are free—within limits—to move and breathe and live the lives they choose.

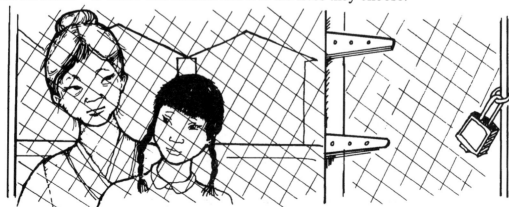

The Golden Gate Bridge

A beautiful and majestic symbol of freedom has stood at the entrance to the San Francisco Bay since 1937. It is the Golden Gate Bridge. The bridge is a symbol of freedom because it, like any bridge, opens up possibilities for travel that were once restricted and even impossible. The bridge also serves as a reminder of the limitless capabilities of human ingenuity, being one of the largest, most encompassing, and most spectacular suspension bridges ever built.

The architectural design of the Golden Gate Bridge is truly masterful. It is 4,200 feet (1,280 meters) long and 90 feet (27 meters) wide. It rises 220 feet (67 meters) above the ocean. Six lanes of traffic plus a sidewalk on either side run the length of the bridge. No wonder the bridge cost 35.5 million dollars to build!

Try the design and construction of a suspension bridge yourself, like the one illustrated above. Use the following as your materials:

- toothpicks
- craft sticks
- glue
- string

Try to make your bridge functional and beautiful. But it is all right to make it much smaller than the Golden Gate Bridge!

Name: _____ Date: _____

The Bombings of Pearl Harbor and Hiroshima

On December 7, 1941, the Japanese launched an air attack on the American naval base at Pearl Harbor, Hawaii. The entire U.S. Pacific Fleet was crippled in the bombing. Four of its eight battleships were sunk within hours, and 200 planes were completely destroyed. People were injured and lives were lost. Americans were outraged.

The Japanese had wanted to keep the U.S. from using its naval powers against them. What the air raid actually served to do was incite the United States into joining with the Allied Powers in war against the Axis Powers (including Japan).

The novel *Journey to Topaz* shows how dismayed Americans were at the attack, and how baffled by the absurdity of the action. However, they soon joined the many other nations already at war for what turned out to be four more years of fighting. The culmination of the ensuing years came when the United States dropped the first atomic bomb ever used in war on Hiroshima, Japan, on August 6, 1945. Two days later, another atomic bomb was dropped on Nagasaki. Japan was defeated, but the cost for all was very high.

From the information in the novel, what does Yuki Sakane think of the attack on Pearl Harbor? What do those around her think, like her family and friends?

Now, given what you know about Yuki by reading the entire novel, what might she have thought about the bombing of Hiroshima? In the space below, write Yuki's journal entry for August 6, 1945. Use the back of the paper if you need more room.

Name: _____ Date: _____

Geographical Locations in the Novel

In the novel *Journey to Topaz,* characters travel to several locations in the western half of the United States. The novel opens in Berkeley, California. Mr. Sakane is taken to Missoula, Montana, and the rest of the family is evacuated to the Tanforan Assembly Center in the San Francisco Bay area. The three in Tanforan are then relocated to Topaz, Utah, and finally the family moves on together to Salt Lake City. Find all of these locations on the map below and circle them.

On the back of this paper, answer in as much detail as you can why you think the United States government relocated and imprisoned all of its West Coast Japanese Americans. What does geography have to do with it? How did fear play a role? Is there any legitimate defense for the action, given the rights of citizens under the U.S. Constitution?

Western United States

Name: _____ Date: _____

Beauty

Many characters in the novel *Journey to Topaz* seek out beauty in the world around them. They find peace in their days and solace in their hearts by noticing and nurturing a world of beauty. To see the beauty is their special talent. It is also their hold on and hope for freedom. While driving to Topaz, they keep the hope that it may be, at least, a pretty place. At first those hopes are dashed at the sight of it. However, each finds something of beauty. Next to each name below, tell what he/she finds.

1. Mr. Kurihara _____

   _____

   _____

2. Mrs. Sukane _____

   _____

   _____

3. Yuki _____

   _____

   _____

4. Mrs. Kurihara _____

   _____

   _____

5. Mr. Toda _____

   _____

   _____

6. Emi _____

   _____

   _____

How is finding beauty a special kind of freedom for each?

_____

_____

_____

Name: _____ Date: _____

Choosing Your Treasures

The entire Sukane family must go through each and every one of their belongings, discarding, selling, and packing as they go. Because they may only travel with a limited number of belongings, they must make decisions about those things that are of the greatest value to them. And some things, like Yuki's beloved dog, Pepper, are not permitted no matter how valuable they are to their owners.

What are the other things Yuki values most? She does not list all of them specifically, but the reader can guess fairly easily what is most important to her.

Now, if you were faced with a situation like Yuki's, which belongings would you take? In the space provided below, list the ten things you treasure most. Next to each, write why it is of value to you.

Treasured Item	Why It Is Valued
1. _____	_____
2. _____	_____
3. _____	_____
4. _____	_____
5. _____	_____
6. _____	_____
7. _____	_____
8. _____	_____
9. _____	_____
10. _____	_____

Name: _____ Date: _____

Making Choices

Ken Sukane must make two important choices in the novel. In each, he must decide between service to others and himself. However, he is free to choose. What does Ken feel about each of the choices listed below? Why does he choose what he does?

The Choice Between Topaz and College

1. What does Ken feel about this choice? _____

   _____

   _____

2. Why does he choose what he does?_____

   _____

   _____

3. What would you do if faced with this decision?

   _____

   _____

The Choice Between the Army and College

1. What does Ken feel about this choice? _____

   _____

   _____

2. Why does he choose what he does?_____

   _____

   _____

3. What would you do if faced with this decision? _____

   _____

   _____

Name: _____ Date: _____

Confinement

Many studies have been done to show the effects of confinement on an individual's mental, emotional, and physical health. Some persons respond more peacefully than others, but for everyone, it is a strain. What is the response of each of the characters listed below to imprisonment in Topaz?

1. Yuki _____

_____

_____

2. Mrs. Sukane _____

_____

_____

3. Ken _____

_____

_____

4. Mr. Sukane _____

_____

_____

5. Emi _____

_____

_____

6. Mr. Kurihara_____

_____

_____

7. Mrs. Kurihara_____

_____

_____

8. Mr. Toda _____

_____

_____

Significant Events of World War II

There were a number of significant events throughout the entirety of World War II. Choose one of them, research it, and report on it to the class. Tell what happened and why the event is significant. Choose the event from this list. (The events given are not necessarily in order.)

1. Invasion of Poland
2. Invasion of Denmark and Norway
3. Evacuation of Dunkerque
4. Occupation of France
5. The Blitz (The Battle of Britain)
6. Invasion of Africa
7. Battle of the Balkans
8. Invasion of the Soviet Union
9. Battle of the Atlantic
10. Bombing of Pearl Harbor
11. Invasion of Italy
12. German Surrender at Stalingrad
13. D-Day (The Normandy Invasion)
14. Bataan Death March
15. Battle of the Bulge
16. Doolittle Raid
17. Battle of the Coral Sea
18. Battle of Midway
19. Landing on Guadalcanal
20. Bombing of Nagasaki
21. Battle of Leyte Gulf
22. Capture of Iwo Jima
23. Hitler's Suicide
24. Capture of Okinawa
25. Bombing of Hiroshima
26. Resignation of Prime Minister Tojo
27. Japanese Surrender

Name: _____ Date: _____

Seeing the Other Side

In her novel *Journey to Topaz,* Yoshiko Uchida is sensitive to the different perspectives of different people. The humblest of characters (and consequently the strongest) are careful to see that there is more than one side to every issue. Because their open-mindedness frees them from anger and blame, they can live a life of hope, making the best of the present situation. Mr. and Mrs. Sukane are excellent examples of people who, though firm in their own beliefs, accept the freedom of others to think and act as they choose.

Read the following situation carefully. When you are finished, take on the perspective of Chris first and then his parents. Tell how you believe each character sees the situation.

Chris is fourteen years old. Walking home from school one afternoon, he spots a small puppy wandering alone down the middle of the street. Instinctively, Chris goes out to the puppy and brings him to the sidewalk. He notices a tag on the puppy. The address on the tag is about a mile away. There is no phone number, so Chris decides to carry the puppy to its home.

When Chris arrives at the puppy's house, there is no one there. He determines to wait until someone comes home. After about fifteen minutes, a car drives up. The owner is grateful; she has been out looking for the lost puppy. She offers Chris a ride home, and he accepts.

When Chris finally makes it to his own home, he is about forty-five minutes late. His parents see him drive up in a stranger's car, and they are angry. They tell him he is foolish for accepting a ride from a stranger. It seems to Chris that they are frightened because of it, but they do not say so. Chris' parents are also angry because the family had plans to go to his younger sister's school play, and it begins in five minutes. Chris knew about it and had committed to being home on time. Without discussion, Chris is placed on restriction. He feels his parents are being unfair, so out of anger and his own hurt feelings, he doesn't bother to tell them the reason he is late. He also believes that the lady who drove him home is trustworthy because she cares so much about her little dog.

That's the story. How do you think Chris and his parents each view what happened? What are their perspectives?

The Other Side

Chris	Chris' Parents

Political Freedom

The Opportunity of
All People to Take Part
in the Governmental
Decision-Making
Process

Speaking Your Mind

Part of political freedom is exercising your right to an opinion. Write a one-page essay taking a stand on one of the following issues.

- Electoral vote

- Death penalty

- Prayer in public schools

- Public health care

- Employment of illegal aliens

- Children "divorcing" their parents

- Abortion

- Parental consent for juveniles to use birth control

- School dress codes

- Government subsidizing of private school tuition

- Gun control

- Inheritance taxes

- Drafting into the armed forces

- Homosexuals in the military

- Conscientious objection to fighting in the military

- Government aid to the homeless

- Government funding of AIDS research

- Legalization of narcotics

- Government financial support of the arts

- Legal protection of endangered species

Name: _____ Date: _____

The National Anthem of the United States

Francis Scott Key wrote the poem "The Star-Spangled Banner" during the War of 1812. From his vantage point aboard a U.S. truce ship in September of 1814, Key witnessed the British bombardment of Fort McHenry in Baltimore Harbor throughout one night. To his joy, the American flag was still flying in the morning. Key proceeded to write the now classic poem and put it to the tune of "To Anacreon in Heaven" (which, interestingly, was an English drinking song of some popularity). In 1931 Key's song was adopted by Congress as the national anthem of the United States.

More recently, a growing number of Americans have become unhappy with the official anthem of the nation. There seem to be two primary reasons for this. First, many find the song very difficult to sing because of its wide scale, challenging notes, and formal vocabulary. Second, some people have objections to the song's basis in war. They want the anthem to reflect the natural beauty and splendor of the United States, not its military power. An often-mentioned replacement for the anthem is "America, the Beautiful." However, a great many people also feel a strong emotional bond to the current anthem and wish to keep it for its familiarity and the spirit of patriotism that it stirs.

Carefully read the words to "The Star-Spangled Banner" on the next page. Think about its meaning and melody. Then, in the space below (and on the back if you need more room) rewrite the song in your own words.

My Interpretation of "The Star-Spangled Banner"

Now answer, how do you feel about the song? Would you like to keep it or change it? Take a class vote.

"The Star-Spangled Banner"

Oh, say can you see by the dawn's early light
What so proudly we hail'd at the twilight's last gleaming,
Whose broad stripes and bright stars through the perilous fight
O'er the ramparts we watch'd were so gallantly streaming?
And the rockets' red glare, the bombs bursting in air,
Gave proof through the night that our flag was still there.
Oh, say does that star-spangled banner yet wave
O'er the land of the free and the home of the brave?

On the shore dimly seen through the mists of the deep,
Where the foe's haughty host in dread silence reposes,
What is it which the breeze, o'er the towering steep,
As it fitfully blows, half conceals, half discloses?
Now it catches the gleam of the morning's first beam,
In full glory reflected now shines in the stream.
'Tis the star-spangled banner, oh, long may it wave
O'er the land of the free and the home of the brave!

And where is that band who so vauntingly swore
That the havoc of war and the battle's confusion
A home and a country should leave us no more?
Their blood has wash'd out their foul footstep's pollution.
No refuge could save the hireling and slave
From the terror of flight or the gloom of the grave,
And the star-spangled banner in triumph doth wave
O'er the land of the free and the home of the brave.

Oh, thus be it ever when freemen shall stand
Between their lov'd home and the war's desolation!
Blest with vict'ry and peace may the heav'n-rescued land
Praise the power that hath made and preserv'd us a nation!
Then conquer we must, when our cause it is just,
And this be our motto, "In God is our Trust,"
And the star-spangled banner in triumph shall wave
O'er the land of the free and the home of the brave.

— *Francis Scott Key*

Name: _____ Date: _____

The Rights of All People

In 1848 at Seneca Falls, New York, Elizabeth Cady Stanton and Lucretia Mott organized the first convention for women's rights. At the convention, the women present wrote what they titled *The Declaration of Sentiments*. It was modelled after *The Declaration of Independence,* rephrased to read, for example, "We hold these truths to be self-evident, that all men and women are created equal . . ."

As a class, read *The Declaration of Independence,* studying how it is written and organized. Then determine the points of your own *The Declaration of Sentiments*. What do you think are the natural rights of all people? Brainstorm your own ideas here. Share them with the class, and then together write your declaration.

Declaration of Sentiments

Name: _____ Date: _____

The Right to Vote and the Constitution

Following are the amendments to the *Constitution of the United States* that pertain to voting. Read these amendments carefully and respond to the questions below.

Amendment 15
(ratified 1870)

Section 1. Right to Vote
The right of citizens of the United States to vote shall not be denied or abridged by the United States or by any State on account of race, color, or previous condition of servitude.

Section 2. Enforcement
The Congress shall have power to enforce this article by appropriate legislation.

Amendment 19
(ratified 1920)

Section 1. Right to Vote
The right of citizens of the United States to vote shall not be denied or abridged by the United States or by any State on account of sex.

Section 2. Enforcement
The Congress shall have power to enforce this article by appropriate legislation.

Amendment 26
(ratified 1971)

Section 1. Right to Vote
The right of citizens of the United States, who are eighteen years of age or older, to vote shall not be denied or abridged by the United States or by any State on account of age.

Section 2. Enforcement
The Congress shall have power to enforce this article by appropriate legislation.

1. Who can vote in the United States? _____

   _____

2. Who cannot?_____

   _____

Provided you are eighteen years of age, you will likely be able to vote one day. Research to find out what steps you will need to take to register to vote. Also, figure out in which year you will first be able to vote for the President of the United States. Presidential elections are held every four years, and there was a presidential election in 1992.

Respond: I will first be eligible to vote for the presidency in _____

Percentages

In any democratic proceeding, it is a majority vote that wins. A majority is made of the portion that exceeds 50% of the vote. In order to determine a majority and the amount of the vote that was cast in each direction, a person should understand percentages. Follow the directions below to determine basic percentages. Then solve the problems on the next page.

To solve per cent problems, change the per cent to a fraction or decimal.

> **1. Changing per cents to fractions:**
>   a. Drop the % symbol.
>   b. Add a denominator of 100; reduce the fraction if possible.
>   Ex: 25% = 25/100 = 1/4
>
> **2. Changing per cents to decimals:**
>   a. Drop the % symbol.
>   b. Add a decimal two places to the left.
>   Ex: 25% = .25

To solve problems where you are trying to get a per cent, change the fraction or decimal to a per cent.

> **1. Changing fractions to per cents:**
>   a. Divide the numerator by the denominator to get a decimal.
>   b. Move the decimal two places to the right and add the % symbol.
>   Ex: 1/4 = .25 = 25%
>
> **2. Changing decimals to per cents:**
>   a. Move the decimal two places to the right and add the % symbol.
>   Ex: .25 = 25%

To solve for any unknown part of a per cent problem use this formula: A = B% of C

> **1. If A is unknown, multiply B by C.**
>   Ex: A = 25% of 12
>   .25 x 12 = 3
>   A = 3
>
> **2. If B is unknown, divide A by C.**
>   Ex: 3 = B% of 12
>   3 ÷ 12 = .25
>   B = 25%
>
> **3. If C is unknown, divide A by B.**
>   Ex: 3 = 25% of C
>   3 ÷ .25 = 12
>   C = 12

Name: _____   Date: _____

Percentages *(cont.)*

Questions	Responses
1. In the last election for mayor, 50% of Cherry Hill's registered voters cast their ballots. There are 12,000 registered voters in Cherry Hill. How many people voted?	
2. Mayor Janine DeFrancis won the election in Cherry Hill. She got 75% of the vote. How many people voted for her?	
3. What percentage of the total number of registered voters voted for Janine DeFrancis?	
4. Four-fifths of Cherry Hill's registered voters are aged 55 or older. How many voters does Cherry Hill have who are 55 or more?	
5. Sunrise Beach residents held a special vote to decide whether or not fireworks would be legal in their town for their upcoming holiday celebrations. 5,225 people voted. Those who voted make up 95% of registered voters. How many registered voters are there in Sunrise Beach?	
6. The voters of Sunrise Beach decided to make fireworks illegal in their town. Those who thought they should be illegal made up 72% of the voters. How many people wanted fireworks to be illegal?	
7. In the Sunrise Beach vote, what percentage of voters wanted to make fireworks legal?	
8. Two-hundred and seventy-five registered voters did not vote in the Sunrise Beach special vote. Those 275 people make up 20% of the voters who first registered to vote in 1993. How many Sunrise Beach voters first registered to vote in 1993?	
9. In Callastoga Falls, 342 people voted for the city council. The number of registered voters is 1,368. What percentage of registered voters voted?	
10. How many people would need to vote in Callastoga Falls order to have 75% of all registered voters vote?	
11. Ignacio Alvarez won the new council seat with 228 votes cast for him. What percentage of the voters voted for him? (Round your answer.)	
12. Ignacio Alvarez's opponent, Alice Piñon, had 114 votes. She needed 115 more to beat Mr. Alvarez. What percentage of the registered voters who did not vote did she need to win this election? (Round your answer.)	

Name: _____   Date: _____

Genetics

When an individual is politically free, he/she has the ability to take part in all decisions that affect the whole. In science, there is a field by which decisions that affect the whole are determined by a few. The field is genetics and the few are called *genes.*

Genes determine nearly everything about an individual's make-up, from the color of that individual's eyes to his/her shoe size. A baby receives genes from the parents. They, in turn, have received their genes from their parents, and so on. This is why members of the same biological family share common characteristics.

Different forms of the same gene are called *alleles.* Some alleles are dominant and some are recessive. For example, the allele for brown eyes is dominant and the allele for blue eyes is recessive. If a person has two blue-eye alleles, that person will have blue eyes. However, that person will have brown eyes if he/she has two brown alleles *or* one brown allele and one blue allele. Blond hair and albinism are two other alleles that are recessive. Recessive traits can only occur if a person has two recessive alleles.

The chart below will show the probability for blond hair in a child born to dark-haired parents who each carry a recessive allele for blond hair.

D = dark hair
B = blond hair

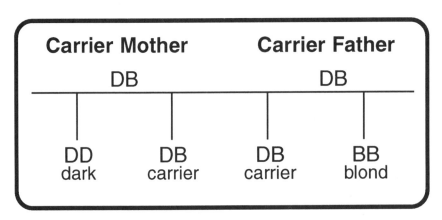

Chances are one in four that a child will have blond hair. Chances are two in four that a child will have dark hair but carry the recessive allele. Chances are one in four that a child will have dark hair with no recessive allele.

Respond:

1. Is there any possibility that a child will have blond hair if one parent has two alleles for dark hair?

2. If each parent carries one allele for albinism and one normal allele, what are the chances that a child of theirs will have albinism?

3. The ability to taste the chemical PTC (phenylthiocarbimide) comes from a dominant allele. If T = the allele for tasting PTC and N = the allele for not tasting PTC, in what two combinations of alleles can a person taste PTC?

4. What combination of alleles must a blue-eyed person have?

5. Make a chart like the one given above showing the possible allele combinations for four children born to one parent who has dark hair with one recessive allele and one parent who has blond hair.

Victory Gardens

During World War II, there was a great rush of patriotic fervor in the United States. People rallied around the causes of the war doing everything they could to help the war effort. Victory Gardens became a common sight. The Victory Garden was an attempt to help in the war effort to produce more food. Troops overseas needed to be fed, and food at home was being rationed. People grew vegetables in any garden space they could find in order to supplement both.

The Victory Garden has come to symbolize an individual's support of the causes of his/her government. As a class, choose a cause that you favor and that your national government supports. Once you have chosen the cause, pick a variety of vegetables that you can grow. Plant the seeds in some available land on the school grounds. Post a sign in the garden stating the cause that you support. Also display your national flag there if you choose. Tend the garden regularly, keeping it watered and weeded. When the vegetables have grown, pick them or dig them up and have a victory celebration.

Here are some gardening tips:

1. Dig up the soil about 12 inches (30 centimeters) down.

2. Break up the soil and mix in fertilizer.

3. Rake the soil smooth before planting.

4. Spread mulch over the planted soil to help prevent weeds and to keep the soil moist.

5. Pinch off a small portion of the top of the main stem to make the plant grow fuller and more productive.

6. Pull up and replant any plants growing too closely together in order to provide each plant ample room to grow.

7. When staking a plant to keep it growing erect, tie it loosely to the stake so that the stem will not be injured.

8. Remember to water and weed regularly!

Designing a Flag

Nations, states, provinces, and private organizations around the world have adopted flags to show reverence and respect for that which they symbolize. Below are some flags and their meanings. After looking at the flags and studying their compositions, turn to the next page and follow the directions there.

Argentina

The stripes are blue and white depicting the colors worn by the soldiers who fought the British in 1806–7. The yellow sun represents the country's freedom from Spain.

Canada

This red and white flag shows a red maple leaf with 11 points. It is the national symbol for Canada.

China

This flag is red with yellow stars. The large star designates the leadership of the communists. The smaller stars depict groups of workers.

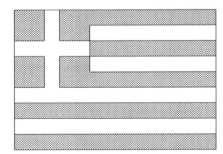

Greece

The blue of the flag represents the sky and the sea. The white represents the purity of Greece's fight for independence. The white cross stands for the Greek Orthodox religion.

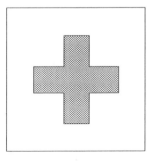

The Red Cross

The red cross on this white flag is a direct symbol for the organization's name. It is also a tribute to Switzerland, where the Red Cross was founded. (The Swiss flag shows a white cross on a red background.) This same society has slightly different flags depending on the nation in which it is located. For example, in Israel the flag shows a red Star of David on a white field and in Muslim countries there is a red crescent centered on a white background.

Name: _____ Date: _____

Designing a Flag *(cont.)*

Choose a place or organization which you respect and value. Research to find if it already has a flag. If so, study its flag.

What is it about this place or organization that you value? Brainstorm your ideas here:

_____   _____

_____   _____

_____   _____

_____   _____

_____   _____

_____   _____

_____   _____

_____   _____

_____   _____

_____   _____

Circle the most important ideas you listed above. Now design a flag of your own using these ideas in symbolic forms. Your image(s) can be simple or complex. Be sure to color your flag, too. Draw and color it here or on the back.

Having Fun With the Scales

It is likely that "Do, Re, Mi, Fa, So, La, Ti, Do" are familiar to you. The notes they represent are called the notes of the musical scale, and they are the basic components of all musical arrangements.

For the movie *The Sound of Music,* Rodgers and Hammerstein wrote a song that rearranges those notes. At one point the characters sing, for example, "Do, Mi, Mi/Mi, So, So/Re, Fa, Fa/La, Ti, Ti." This was the way the lead character had of teaching the other characters how to sing. She sang, "When you know the notes to sing/You can sing most anything." She's right.

Learn and study the notes of the musical scale. Get familiar with each. Now, have some fun with them! Cut out all the notes at the bottom of the page. (The second "Do" represents the highest note; there is an asterisk marked next to it.) Rearrange them in any order you like, gluing them down. Remember, you have the freedom to choose, so do anything you want! Now practice singing your new arrangement. Can you do it? Can someone else sing it with you and carry the same tune? Now try singing someone else's tune. Do your new songs sound "right" or do they sound strange? Can you rearrange them differently to make them sound better? Would you like to add or delete any notes? Give it a try.

Do	Do	Do	Do	Do	Do	Do
Re	Re	Re	Re	Re	Re	Re
Mi	Mi	Mi	Mi	Mi	Mi	Mi
Fa	Fa	Fa	Fa	Fa	Fa	Fa
So	So	So	So	So	So	So
La	La	La	La	La	La	La
Ti	Ti	Ti	Ti	Ti	Ti	Ti
Do*	Do*	Do*	Do*	Do*	Do*	Do*

"Yankee Doodle" and Other War Songs

Times of war tend to be times of great patriotic fervor. Often, many new songs come out of war that boost morale and join people in a common spirit. One of the most popular and long-lasting war songs is "Yankee Doodle." It was written before the American Revolutionary War by a British Army doctor named Richard Schuckburg. He wrote it to make fun of the farmers and common people who were gathering haphazardly to fight. However, the people he wanted to offend took the song as their own and sang it with pride. They believed in their cause and were not about to let anyone's jokes stop them. The original song goes like this:

Yankee Doodle

Father and I went down to camp
Along with Captain Goodin,
And there we saw the men and boys
As thick as hasty puddin'.

Chorus: Yankee Doodle keep it up,
Yankee Doodle dandy,
Mind the music and the step,
And with the girls be handy.

And there was Captain Washington
Upon a slappin' stallion,
And all the men and boys around,
I guess there was a million.

Chorus

Yankee Doodle went to town
Ridin' on a pony,
Stuck a feather in his cap
And called it macaroni.

Chorus

Many more verses have been added over the years, so today there are several variations of the song.

Many other songs exist. Research to find out about one other war song, who wrote it, why it was written, and what it meant to the people singing it.

Apple Pie (er...Crisp)

In the United States, a common patriotic expression is "It's as American as apple pie." Apple pies are wholesome and good, and so is America to the American way of thinking. The apple pie has become a symbol for this belief.

One of the ways Americans celebrate their political freedom is by baking and eating apple pies. It is especially good as part of a Fourth of July celebration. Because apple pie can be a little complex, try the recipe below for apple crisp to see how good an "apple pie" can be!

Ingredients:

1 medium-sized cooking apple

1 tablespoon (15 mL) water

1 ½ tablespoons (25 mL) all-purpose flour

1 tablespoon (15 mL) sugar

1 tablespoon (15 mL) butter, softened

¼ teaspoon (1 mL) cinnamon

Directions:

Heat the oven to 350° Fahrenheit (180°C). Pare and slice the apple to make about 1 cup. Place the sliced apple into a 10-ounce (300 gm) custard cup. Sprinkle the water over the apple. Mix the remaining ingredients together with a fork until they are crumbly. Sprinkle this mixture over the apple. Bake the apple crisp uncovered at 350°F (180°C) for 25–30 minutes, or until the apple is soft and the topping is golden-brown.

Name: _____ Date: _____

How to Become President of the United States

The Constitution of the United States clearly outlines the requirements an individual must satisfy to be elected President. The Constitution reads:

> *"No person except a natural-born citizen, or a citizen of the United States at the time of the adoption of this Constitution, shall be eligible to the office of President; neither shall any person be eligible to that office who shall not have attained to the age of thirty-five years, and been fourteen years as a resident within the United States."*

In other words, to be President, a person must be born a U.S. citizen, be thirty-five or older, and have lived in the United States for fourteen years. Given these requirements, who of the following people are free to seek the office of President? (You will probably have to do some research.)

Candidate	Born a Citizen?	Age?	Years of Residence?	May Run for President?
1. Gloria Steinem				
2. H. Norman Schwarzkopf				
3. Wilma Mankiller				
4. Corazon Aquino				
5. Bill Cosby				
6. Princess Diana				
7. Macauley Culkin				
8. Arnold Schwarzenegger				
9. Maya Angelou				
10. You				

Name: _____ Date: _____

Everyone's a Referee!

Imagine: What would it be like if sports were completely democratic —if everyone had a say in all the rules? For example, while playing basketball what if…

- Everyone voted for who got the ball first, instead of having a jump shot?
- Every time a referee blew the whistle, all players and the audience voted?
- Not only the referee but *every player* had a whistle?

Write: What do you think a game like the one described above would be like? Describe it here. Use the back if you need more room.

_____

_____

_____

_____

_____

_____

_____

_____

_____

_____

_____

_____

_____

_____

_____

_____

_____

Play: Choose a sport and play it, but this time make every player a referee or umpire, too. Everyone will vote on a referee's call.

Discuss: Did what you think would happen really happen? Was it fun to play this way, or was it frustrating? Which way do you prefer to play?

Nothing But the Truth: A Documentary Novel

by Avi (Orchard Books, 1991)

(Available in Canada, Gage Dist.; UK, Baker & Taylor Int.; Australia, Franklin Watts)

Summary: This very creative novel takes a unique approach to storytelling. The story unfolds in documentary style—letters, transcripts, journal entries, memos—and the reader is left to judge for him/herself the actions of each character. We see clearly the things left unsaid, misunderstandings and how they happen, erroneous assumptions, and the true motives behind behaviors. Every character is fully human, making mistakes along the way, and butting heads against the all-too-human desire to control the actions of others. The reader is given the opportunity to see that there is always more than one side to every story. The reader might also learn something about his/her own poor communications.

Philip Malloy, a ninth grader at Harrison High School, loves to run, is interested in girls, enjoys math, and hates literature. Running on the track team is the most important thing in life to him. Reading *The Call of the Wild* for Miss Narwin's English class is perhaps the least important. But Philip doesn't realize until too late that he needs a grade of C or better in all of his classes in order to join the track team. The coach and team want him very much, because track is truly where Philip's talent is, but there is no getting around the rule. Philip believes that Miss Narwin just does not like him. After all, his charm and sense of humor work on everyone else, so why not her?

The problem is this: Miss Narwin cares very much about Philip and truly wants him to succeed; however, she sees his humor as disrespect. Respect for her and the literature she loves is very important to Miss Narwin. What Philip does not see is her genuine concern for the learning of all her students.

The difficulties between the two escalate when Philip is switched to Miss Narwin's homeroom in the spring semester. Philip hums along with the playing of the national anthem before the morning announcements. The school rules clearly state that students will stand at respectful, silent attention when the anthem is played. But in Philip's previous homeroom there had been a lot of talking and joking during the music, particularly from the teacher himself. Philip is confused by Miss Narwin's adamant insistence that he remain silent, and she assumes that he is just being disruptive and intentionally rude.

Both characters take their concerns to other people. What then evolves for each is a series of miscommunications, twisted words, and unpleasant experiences that grow far larger than they warrant, and certainly much bigger than either Miss Narwin or Philip intends. Eventually, after Philip's suspension for disobedience, the unresolved personal issues of the two reach the national media. The reactions of those around them and the decisions that each needs to make only serve to bury the two in a seemingly hopeless mire of misunderstanding and emotional pain. What was certainly avoidable becomes tragic for the both of them.

Avi is consistently fair to all characters. He remains objective, showing all sides to the story, and thereby encouraging the reader to think through all sides. Who is right and who is wrong fall by the wayside. Of greater interest becomes the desire to create a winning situation for all, because the miscommunications that result from the present situation only serve to injure everyone involved.

Name: _____ Date: _____

Communication

In order to be heard politically, we need to know how to communicate effectively. For various reasons, Philip Malloy and Miss Narwin of Avi's *Nothing But the Truth* fail to do that with one another.

Below is the beginning of a feigned conversation between Philip and Miss Narwin. Giving each character at least five turns to speak, how would you complete the conversation? Have the characters speak as they do in the novel.

Miss Narwin: Class, as you have just read in Shakespeare's play *Julius Caesar,* Caesar feels betrayed by the actions of a good friend. Philip, what are you doing? What's that book you're reading?

Philip: *The Outsiders . . .*

_____

_____

_____

_____

_____

_____

_____

_____

_____

_____

_____

_____

_____

_____

_____

_____

_____

_____

_____

Name: _____ Date: _____

Slanted Reporting

There is a suggestion in the novel that some of the reporting done about Philip's suspension is slanted. That is, only his side of the story is told. Is this true? Is there any attempt to learn the other side of the story? Answer here.

_____

_____

_____

_____

Read the following newspaper article. Below it, write whether or not you think the article is slanted or if it is, in fact, an objective piece of reporting. If you do think it is slanted, what perspective is missing?

San Diego, CA – In responding to a call late Wednesday afternoon, police discovered two young children left unattended in their home. The girl and boy, aged three and five, were preparing lunch for themselves when the police arrived. A neighbor said she had recently begun to suspect that the children were left alone every day while their father, a single parent, was at work; however, she hesitated to call authorities until she knew for sure. The neighbor also said the children's father comes home several hours late at least two nights a week. Pending a police investigation, formal charges have not been made.

Response to San Diego News Item

_____

_____

_____

_____

_____

_____

_____

_____

_____

_____

_____

Challenge: Find articles in your local paper and discuss whether or not they are objective.

Name: _____ Date: _____

Inside Philip

Throughout the novel, the reader gets greater insight into the character of Philip Malloy at every turn of events. The more the reader knows about him—or any character—the more that reader can understand his actions. Next to each date and time below, write what you learn or surmise about Philip from the documentation that follows it in the novel.

1. Thursday, March 15, 11:05 PM

2. Friday, March 16, 8:20 PM

3. Friday, March 23, 10:30 PM

4. Monday, March 26, 1:30 PM

5. Friday, March 30, 8:05 AM

6. Sunday, April 1, 9:50 AM

7. Tuesday, April 3, 7:40 AM

8. Tuesday, April 3, 12:30 PM

9. Wednesday, April 4, 8:55 AM

10. Monday, April 9, 8:30 AM

Respond: Is Philip free to speak for himself at his school?

Does he have the freedom to take part in the decisions that affect him?

Name: _____ Date: _____

Effective Communication

Having read the novel, a reader is not likely to say that Miss Narwin is a liar. She is very honest about her perspective. However, it might be said that she does not always communicate effectively. Sometimes she leaves important information unsaid, and the reader can only assume her reasons why. For example, when the reporter, Jennifer Stewart, calls her for her side of the story, Miss Narwin chooses not to speak. Perhaps even more detrimental to her is her lack of communication directly with Philip at the outset of the problem. She does not do anything wrong—she follows all proper channels—yet Philip never knows what her thoughts and perspective are. At one point, she suggests to her sister that she will have a heart-to-heart talk with him, but, unfortunately, that never happens.

If Miss Narwin spoke honestly and openly with Philip Malloy, what might she tell him? Write it out.

"Philip, I want you to know that . . . _____

_____

_____

_____

_____

_____

_____

_____

_____

_____

_____

_____

_____

Respond: If you were Philip Malloy, how would you feel about a teacher telling you such things as you had Miss Narwin say above?

_____

_____

_____

_____

Name: _____ Date: _____

Questions from the Novel

Answer each of the questions below. Use examples from the novel to support your response whenever it is reasonable to do so.

1. Is Mr. Malloy a good listener? _____

_____

_____

2. Is Dr. Doane a liar? _____

_____

_____

3. Is Dr. Seymour two-faced? _____

_____

_____

4. Is Philip Malloy disrespectful? _____

_____

_____

5. Does Allison Doresett make assumptions? _____

_____

_____

6. Is Dr. Palleni a good disciplinarian? _____

_____

_____

7. Is Ken Barchet a good friend? _____

_____

_____

Respond: Was it difficult to answer some of the questions asked above? Why or why not?

_____

_____

Name: _____ Date: _____

Why Are They Acting That Way?

In the novel *Nothing But the Truth,* many characters assume things about Philip's feelings based on his behavior and the judgments they hear from others. Read each scenario given below, and under each, answer the question given.

1. Four-year-old Jamie bit her twelve-year-old brother when he came home from school. He had not said or done anything to her from the time he came in the door. Afterwards, her brother pushed her away. She cried and told their mother that he had pushed her. Jamie's mother told her to go outside and play because she was too busy to listen just now.

   ➥ Why do you think Jamie bit her brother? _____

   _____

   _____

2. The last time Pete and Shana went out on a date, they had a really good time. They laughed a lot together. In fact, they were having so much fun that they forgot the time, and Shana got home an hour late. They were supposed to go out again this weekend, but Shana just called Pete to tell him she can't go. When he asked her why not, she just said she didn't feel like it.

   ➥ Why do you think Shana called off the date? _____

   _____

   _____

3. Carlton's parents have had an argument every night this week. Each night when his mother got home from work, she went silently up to her room. Carlton's father, who is unemployed right now, usually followed her up. Carlton heard them arguing, but he could not hear what they were saying. It bothered him, and he imagined all sorts of things that they were fighting about.

   ➥ What do you think Carlton's parents were fighting about?_____

   _____

   _____

Now share your answers with the class. Use tally marks below to total how many different answers you have. Discuss. Can you ever really know by assuming?

Different answers to number 1:_____

Different answers to number 2:_____

Different answers to number 3:_____

Name: _____ Date: _____

Errors in Judgment

Describe one time, if any, that you think each of the following characters made an error in judgment.

1. Philip Malloy _____

_____

_____

2. Miss Narwin _____

_____

_____

3. Dr. Doane _____

_____

_____

4. Dr. Palleni_____

_____

_____

5. Dr. Seymour _____

_____

_____

6. Mr. Malloy _____

_____

_____

7. Mrs. Malloy _____

_____

_____

8. Allison Doresett _____

_____

_____

9. Coach Jamison _____

_____

_____

10. Jennifer Stewart _____

_____

_____

Name: _____ Date: _____

Drawing Parallels

The novel *Nothing But the Truth* is full of parallels between the experiences of Philip and Miss Narwin. The author, Avi, even goes so far as to have them say the exact same things in their separate responses to the same situation.

The parallels show the reader how tragic it is that the individuals feel the same way and could likely help one another, but they do not communicate their shared feelings to each other. Both Miss Narwin and Philip want to be heard and valued, but neither really gets those needs met.

List here as many parallels as you can find between Philip Malloy and Margaret Narwin.

_____

_____

_____

_____

_____

_____

_____

_____

_____

_____

_____

_____

_____

_____

_____

_____

_____

_____

Respond:

1. What do you learn about each character from these parallels? _____

   _____

2. How do both Philip and Miss Narwin restrict their own freedom by keeping silent? _____

   _____

Name: _____ Date: _____

Understanding Both Sides

As the reader sees in *Nothing But the Truth,* there are always two sides to every situation. The blacks and whites of life are not as distinct as we sometimes like to think. There is often a gray area where no one is right and no one is wrong. People are just doing the best they can with what they know.

For any three of the situations given below, write down two opposite ways of looking at each. Then suggest a third alternative that may be the gray area discussed above.

1. Trying juveniles as adults

2. Contraceptives for teenagers

3. Using lab animals for scientific experiments

4. Masculine and feminine socialization for boys and girls

5. Wearing uniforms at school

6. Eating meat and animal products

7. Taking a day off from school without being sick

Situation Number	Side 1	Side 2	Gray Area

Choose one of the above topics about which you have written. Join in a small group with others who have written on the same topic. Discuss, and appoint a secretary to take notes. Present your discussion to the class.

Extension I: Are you free to make your own decisions about each of the above? Explain.

Extension II: As a class, vote on the above topics. If your class were the law-making group on these topics, how would they fare? Are you in agreement with each of these "laws"?

Number the Stars

by Lois Lowry (Houghton Mifflin, 1989)

(Available in Canada, Thomas Allen & Son; UK, Lions; Australia, Jackaranda Wiley)

Summary: Annemarie Johansen and Ellen Rosen are both normal, healthy, ten-year-old girls in the fall of 1943. They live in the same apartment building in Copenhagen, Denmark, and are the best of friends. Though Ellen is Jewish and Annemarie is Lutheran, they share a love and respect for one another that allows them to celebrate the other's differences and enjoy all the more what they have in common. Yet there is one more thing they share. They have both lived under Nazi occupation in their country since 1940, and things seem to be getting worse.

The two girls have grown accustomed to the presence of soldiers on the street corners, to the rationing of electricity, to the lack of meat, butter, and sugar in their homes, and so much more. But one day when the Rosen family goes to synagogue to celebrate the Jewish new year, they and the rest of the congregation are told that the Nazis have taken the temple's roster of synagogue members, and that all Jews will be "relocated" at any time. The Rosens hurry home to plan their escape.

Mr. and Mrs. Rosen go into hiding, leaving their daughter, Ellen, to stay with the Johansens as one of their own. She pretends to be Annemarie's now deceased sister, Lise, who died three years earlier in an auto accident. Lise, at the time of her death, was going to marry Peter Nielsen. Annemarie still sees Peter occasionally, but he is no longer the fun-loving young man he once was; now he is usually serious and always hurried. Unknown to her, Peter will play an important part in what happens to all of the Rosens next.

One day shortly after the Rosens leave, Mrs. Johansen takes her own daughters as well as Ellen to her brother Henrik's house by the seashore. Henrik is a fisherman. Things begin to happen there that Annemarie does not understand. Most particularly, in Henrik's house they hold a wake for Annemarie's Great-aunt Birte. The problem is that Annemarie never had a Great-aunt Birte, and she knows it. Several people she has never seen before come to the wake, and then in comes Peter Nielsen. Suddenly, Mr. and Mrs. Rosen also appear. Last of all to come are German soldiers wondering why so many have gathered together. Mrs. Johansen fools them with the story of the dead aunt, but after they leave, the coffin is opened to reveal coats and blankets for everyone at the wake. They are all Jews and are going to be hidden on Uncle Henrik's fishing boat to cross the sea to Sweden, which is still a free country. In the dead of night they make their way to the boat.

Crucial to their escape is a handkerchief coated in a revolutionary drug designed by the Danish Resistance, of which Peter is a key member. In time we learn also that Lise really died as a member of the Resistance. The new drug they have developed deadens the smelling capabilities of search dogs employed by the Nazis to find people hidden on the boats. Annemarie's bravery and quick thinking are the only things that get the handkerchief to Uncle Henrik in time. The Rosens and the others are delivered safely to Sweden.

Two years later, the war is over and the Danes are free. The Johansens await eagerly the return of the Rosens, and Annemarie vows to wear the Star of David necklace Ellen left behind until the day when she sees her friend again.

98

Name: _____

Date: _____

Different and the Same

Use the Venn diagram on this page to compare and contrast the characteristics of Ellen and Annemarie, pointing out their physical, social, and personal similarities and differences.

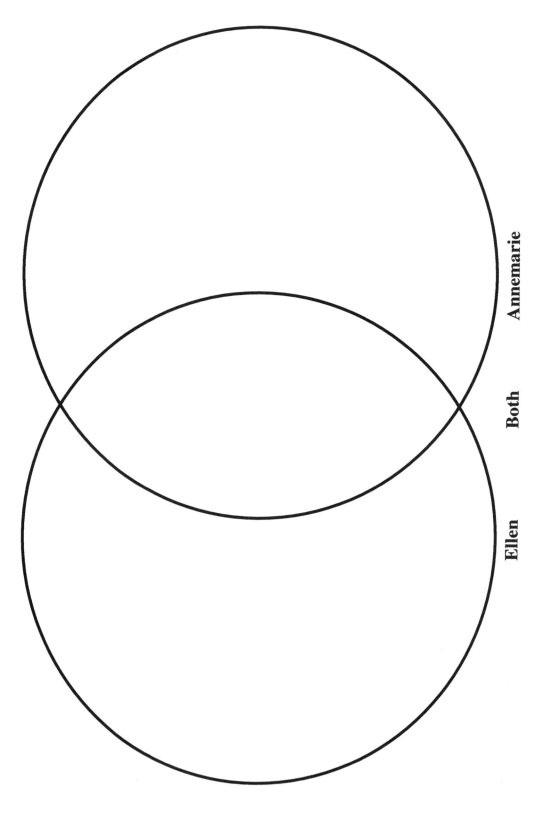

Ellen   Both   Annemarie

Name: _____ Date: _____

"Numbers the Stars"

In chapter 10 the author quotes the biblical passage from which the title comes. It reads, in part,

It is he who heals the broken in spirit
and binds up their wounds,
he who numbers the stars one by one...

Annemarie questions the words of this quote. She wonders how anyone can count the stars. The sky, in fact the world, is just too big and scary. She feels unsafe and very small.

Reread this passage in chapter 10 of the novel. Then write in your own words what you think the phrase "numbers the stars" means and why you think the author chose it.

What I Think the Phrase Means

_____

_____

_____

_____

_____

_____

_____

_____

Why I Think Lois Lowry Chose the Phrase

_____

_____

_____

_____

_____

_____

_____

_____

Name: _____ Date: _____

"An Ideal of Human Decency"

In the afterward, Lois Lowry tells of a real young man named Kim Malthe-Bruun on whom the character Peter Nielsen may be based. Kim, though very young like Peter, fought in the resistance to stop the Nazis in any way possible. He, too, was captured and executed at the age of twenty-one.

As Lowry tells us, on the night before he was killed, Kim wrote a letter home to his mother. In this letter he admonished her to preserve a new dream, and he said,

. . . but the dream for you all, young and old, must be to create an ideal of human decency, and not a narrow-minded and prejudiced one.

Kim and Peter gave their lives for this "ideal of human decency." What do you think Kim meant by it? Think about what he meant, and then write your own ideal of human decency here. You can brainstorm your ideas on the back of this paper before you begin writing.

My Ideal of Human Decency

Name: _____ Date: _____

The Resistance

There truly was a Danish Resistance, and as the novel tells us, they were "Danish people—no one knew who, because they were very secret—who were determined to bring harm to the Nazis however they could." Often members of the Resistance were very young, and as the author tells us, we can be quite sure that they were all very brave.

In *Number the Stars* we meet two members of the Danish Resistance, Lise Johansen and Peter Nielsen. Both are executed because of their work, Lise by car and Peter by firing squad. Under each name written below, brainstorm the things you know about each character, both externally and internally. (This can also be done as a class.)

Lise

_____

_____

_____

_____

_____

_____

Peter

_____

_____

_____

_____

_____

_____

Imagine other members of the Resistance. What do you think they were like? Create two characters below from your own imagination who you think might have been part of the Resistance. (You can discuss this as a class before creating your own characters.)

Character A

_____

_____

_____

_____

_____

_____

Character B

_____

_____

_____

_____

_____

_____

Now think about all four characters, Lise, Peter, and the two you have created. Imagine them attending the meeting that Lise and Peter attended just before she was killed. What do you think they were saying? What were they doing? On the back of this paper write a script of at least 10 lines that you think might have taken place at this meeting of the Danish Resistance. Share in small groups or with the class.

Name: _____ Date: _____

To Have and Have Not

Under Nazi occupation, the Danes lose a great many things they once had. Mrs. Johansen misses coffee and tea, Mr. Johansen misses cigarettes, Kirsti would dearly love a pink-frosted cupcake, and Annemarie is delighted at the thought of butter, milk, and cream. The novel goes on to tell us of many other things the Danes are without or that are being rationed. List here all the things mentioned that you can think of.

_____   _____   _____
_____   _____   _____
_____   _____   _____
_____   _____   _____
_____   _____   _____

Along with these material things, the political takeover of Denmark has also left the people lacking in many of their political, social, and, in fact, human freedoms. Use your creativity and insight to list at least ten such things that the Danes are missing.

1. _____

2. _____

3. _____

4. _____

5. _____

6. _____

7. _____

8. _____

9. _____

10. _____

11. _____

12. _____

Share your ideas with the class and discuss.

Name: _____ Date: _____

King Christian X

Christian X (1870–1947) was the king of Denmark from 1912 until his death shortly after the events of this novel. He is best remembered today as a symbol for the Danish Resistance during the second world war.

Christian X, as *Number the Stars* makes clear, was a well-loved and well-respected monarch. The people felt that he always had their good in mind. Indeed, he made it his business to better the lives of those he governed through new laws, social reform, and a constitutional change that put an end to the special rights of the upper classes.

Though King Christian surrendered to the invading Germans, he never complied with their tactics. He continued to occupy the throne throughout their occupation of his country, though he was held captive in the palace from 1943–1945.

In the second chapter of the novel, Lois Lowry relates a story about Christian X that is dear to the hearts of Danes everywhere. Respond to the following questions about that story and then discuss your ideas with the class.

1. Why is the story so special to the Danes?

2. What does the story mean?

3. What does the story have to do with political freedom?

Name: _____ Date: _____

Map of Locations from the Novel

Below is a map showing all the areas of significance to the novel. Locate and highlight (or otherwise mark) the following:

Denmark, Norway, Holland, Belgium, France, Sweden, Germany

Northern Europe

Name: _____ Date: _____

The Swastika

In modern times when we see the swastika, we tend to think of the Nazi party of Germany, as well as others who wish to mirror themselves in the Nazi image. The symbol is not a favorable one, but rather one of many negative connotations. However, it was not always so. Actually, the swastika is an ancient religious symbol depicting good luck and blessings. It dates back to the European Bronze Age, and is still used in China, Japan, India, Persia, and among the Indians of North, Central, and South America. The Nazis standardized the swastika to show the bent arms of the cross pointing in a clockwise direction; however, traditionally the arms are bent either clockwise or counterclockwise. Below are several examples of the swastika.

North American Indian   **Pima Indian**   **Siberian**   **Nazi**

There are many other symbols that have both negative and positive connotations, depending on who is using them and how they are being used. Perhaps none is so emotionally charged as the swastika, but that, as with beauty, is truly in the eyes of the beholder. Think about each of the symbols given below. Then describe a time and place when each might be considered as a positive and a time and place when each is thought to be negative. There are no right and wrong answers. Just write what you think. Then discuss with your class.

Symbol	Positive Time and Place	Negative Time and Place
1. United States flag		
2. a skeleton		
3. a white rose		
4. the color red		
5. a clenched fist		

The Star of David

The Star of David, or Shield of David, is the universal symbol depicting Judaism. It can be found anywhere that has an association with the Jewish faith, including synagogues, Jewish organizations, and the flag of Israel.

The star is made of two triangles which interconnect. They form a star of six points. Often the star is colored gold or blue.

The star as a symbol of Judaism dates back to at least A.D. 200 when the term *Magen David* (Shield of David) first came to be recorded. The symbol itself first appears as early as 960 B.C., making it one of the oldest symbols still in use today.

Cut out the two triangles below and interweave them to make a Star of David, as shown. Research to find out the significance of the star to the Jewish faith.

Social Freedom

The Opportunity
to Live, Worship, Speak,
Work, and Interrelate as
One Chooses

Name: _____ Date: _____

Using Slang

Slang is a common spoken language choice for many young people. In brief, it is language that is colloquial and familiar, but normally thought of as below the level of standard language. Look up the meaning of slang in your dictionary to extend your understanding of its definition. Then do the following activities.

1. Brainstorm all the slang you know that you think is appropriate to share with the class. Think of all the slang you have heard but is not common today, like "groovy" or "far out." At home, ask your parents or grandparents about the slang they used when they were children or teenagers. Add these words to your list.

   _____   _____   _____

   _____   _____   _____

   _____   _____   _____

   _____   _____   _____

   _____   _____   _____

   _____   _____   _____

   _____   _____   _____

   _____   _____   _____

   _____   _____   _____

   _____   _____   _____

   _____   _____   _____

   _____   _____   _____

   _____   _____   _____

2. Share all the words you thought of with the class. Make a class master list.

3. Try to find a dictionary that lists at least some of these words.

4. Make your own class dictionary of slang. List the words alphabetically, grouping them by initial letter. Try to include pronunciation guides if you can. Make the definitions clear and simple.

5. Rewrite a familiar story, like a fairy or folk tale, using slang. (For example: *Way back when, there were these two kids—Hansel and Gretel. Their place was really uncool, and their old lady was always dissin' them. She tried to psych them out and lose them in the woods, but Hansel was a sharp little dude who bagged her plans . . . .)*

Name: _____ Date: _____

Using Slang II

In small groups, come up with new slang terms for each of the common words listed below along with others of your choice. Keep in mind that slang usually comes from standard words that are simply used in new ways.

Formal Terms	Slang Terms
1. good	
2. bad	
3. clean	
4. messy	
5. young	
6. serious	
7. mischievous	
8. loud	
9. delicious	
10. expensive	
11. funny	
12. friendly	
13.	
14.	
15.	
16.	
17.	
18.	
19.	
20.	
21.	
22.	

Name: _____ Date: _____

Filling Out a Job Application

For good or for bad, part of social freedom is having the income to make choices possible. Usually, adults need to have employment in order to have an income. High-paying jobs often require the submission of a resume. A resume usually lists a person's name and address, education, work history, and references to be contacted for a description of the person's value as an employee. Jobs of low to average incomes often require the submission of a job application. Job applications can be picked up at the desired place of employment. They should always be filled in neatly so that all information is easy to read. Also, a neat and careful application suggests to the future employer that the applicant is also that way.

As a class, choose a "pretend" job for which all of you will apply. This should be a job that would be reasonable for each of you to hold at your age and level of experience and education. Now, to the best of your ability fill in the application here and on the next page, keeping in mind that it is for the job in question. Then share your applications in small groups. Give each other honest feedback about your application appearance and information. How can you help each other improve your applications? Share a few with the class.

Application for Employment

Position: _____

Personal

Name:_____

                         Last   First   Middle

Date: _____

Street Address _____

City _____ State _____ Zip Code _____

Home Telephone _____ Social Security Number _____

Have you ever applied for employment with us before?

❑ Yes ❑ No   If yes, name the month and year. _____

Are you seeking to work part-time or full-time? Part-time_____ Full-time_____

Do you have any special training or skills (languages, computer knowledge, etc.)?

_____

_____

Do you have any relatives or friends we are currently employing or have employed in the past? (List names and relationships)

_____

_____

Do you have any physical conditions that may limit your ability to perform this job?

_____

When are you available to begin employment? _____

Filling Out a Job Application *(cont.)*

Application for Employment

Education

School Name	Location	No. of Years Completed	Did You Graduate?
College _____	_____	_____	_____
High School _____	_____	_____	_____
Elementary School _____	_____	_____	_____
Other _____	_____	_____	_____

List any awards or achievements worth note during your educational experience.

_____

_____

Employment History

Company Name and Address	Position	From Mo/Yr To Mo/Yr	Why did you leave?
_____	_____	_____	_____
_____	_____	_____	_____
_____	_____	_____	_____
_____	_____	_____	_____
_____	_____	_____	_____
_____	_____	_____	_____

Character References *(other than relatives)*

Name	Relationship	Address/Phone Number
_____	_____	_____
_____	_____	_____
_____	_____	_____
_____	_____	_____
_____	_____	_____

Additional Comments_____

The information provided in this application for employment is true and complete. I understand that the completion of this application is not an offer of employment, and that if employed, either the employer or myself may terminate the employment. I give my permission to investigate any of the information included in this application.

Signature _____

Name: _____ Date: _____

Paying Bills

With social freedom comes social responsibility. One of the most basic of these responsibilities is the paying of bills for services rendered. Bill paying is actually very simple, as long as an individual's finances are in order and he/she pays bills in a timely fashion.

Below you will find a mock sample of a bill from a phone company. Read over the charges carefully, check the calculations (sometimes mistakes are made!), and enter the amount you are paying. Most bills require that the entire amount due is paid. With a few there are exceptions, but they usually involve interest (a percentage of the total cost owed to be paid in addition to the full amount of the bill).

Green Bay Phone Company
P.O. Box 11 Green Bay, WI 59230

To: A. Favreau   **Account Number:** 414-639-4286

Monthly Service **$15.00**

Toll Charges

414-653-9209	Appleton, WI	11/3	8 min.	.40
414-841-3286	Manitowac, WI	11/3	23 min.	1.15
414-653-9209	Appleton, WI	11/3	10 min.	.50
414-629-1311	Marinette, WI	11/8	45 min.	2.25
414-841-3286	Manitowac, WI	11/25	13 min.	.65

Total Toll Charges **$4.95**

Long Distance Charges

319-984-3210	Davenport, IA	11/5	63 min.	9.48
708-430-1926	Oak Brook, IL	11/19	12 min.	3.07
714-536-3360	Anaheim, CA	11/25	29 min.	8.89
519-260-3419	London, ONT	11/25	14 min.	6.85

Total Long Distance Charges **$28.29**

Tax and Surcharges **$5.60**

Total Charges for 11/1-11/30 . . . . **$53.48**

Due and payable by 12/15   **Amount Enclosed $** _____

Respond:

1. What call costs the most per minute? _____

2. What calls cost the least per minute? _____

3. Where would you send payment for this bill? _____

Name: _____ Date: _____

Writing Bills

Sometimes it happens that a person is not the one paying the bill, but is instead the one charging for services rendered. This person will need to provide the customer with a bill showing the following:

- customer name and account number
- worker or company name
- individual charges
- taxes

- total charges
- date due
- location where payment can be sent

Given the costs involved for each of the two situations listed below, write bills that clearly show all of the above. Write them up in any way that makes sense to you. Once completed, exchange with a partner and see if they make sense to him/her.

1. J.C. Johnson has his own cleaning service headquartered at 11 Route 6, Brigham, CA 96803. Recently he cleaned the MacKenzie home. His normal charge to clean their house is $25.00. He also charges $10.00 for each special service requested. This time the MacKenzies requested to have their downstairs windows cleaned, the inside of their oven cleaned and polished, and their refrigerator cleaned out. Mr. Johnson includes tax (5%) as part of the basic cleaning fee.

Johnson Cleaning

2. Susan Nishigaya owns her own catering company. She works out of her home at 642 Plaza Drive, Middletown, WY 78429. Recently she catered a wedding for 125 guests. The cost of the meal per guest was $17.00. She also provided the cake and champagne at a cost of $5.00 per guest. For bills of this size, she charges a 10% gratuity on the entire amount. Taxes in her area are 7.75% (but she does not include the gratuity in the amount taxed).

Nishigaya Catering

Name: _____ Date: _____

Restricted Worlds

Read the short story by Ray Bradbury called "All Summer in a Day." (This story can be found in many collections, one of which is *The Stories of Ray Bradbury,* Knopf, 1980.) It describes a world where the sun shines for just one hour every seven years. While reading, imagine the world that Bradbury has created. What do you think it looks like, smells like, feels like, sounds like?

Now, in small groups, read each of the following and imagine in scientific terms what a world with those conditions would be like, with human beings as they are now as the inhabitants. Describe it in writing. Afterwards, share your ideas with the class.

   1. There is no oxygen in the air . . .

   2. Dinosaurs are alive . . .

   3. The current population triples overnight . . .

   4. Rain falls once every seven years, but only for one hour . . .

   5. Earthquakes throughout the world divide all pieces of land into 1 mile/1 kilometer square islands . . .

Name: _____ Date: _____

Social Restrictions

What are the social restrictions on each of the following? In other words, where is their freedom naturally limited? You will need to use your imagination to consider the possibilities that are out of their reach.

1. ant

_____

2. elephant

_____

3. cocker spaniel

_____

4. mouse

_____

5. sparrow

_____

6. goldfish

_____

7. humpback whale

_____

8. jackrabbit

_____

9. rattlesnake

_____

10. human being

Symbols of Freedom

There are many universal symbols for freedom, as well as some that are more personal. On pages 118–119, you will find patterns for common symbols. You can use these patterns for some of the projects described below, if desired.

1. Diorama

A diorama is a miniature scene depicting a moment in time from fiction or real life. To make a diorama, take a long box (like a shoe box) and remove the lid. Cut a hole of about 1/2 inch (1.3 centimeters) in diameter in the center of one short side. This side will be the front of the scene.

 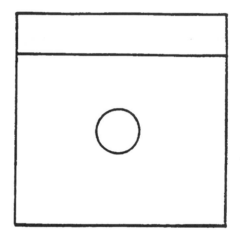

Choose a scene to depict that captures a moment in the celebration of social freedom. It can be a scene of people worshipping in a church, enjoying a cultural holiday, taking part in a family custom, or anything else you can think of that demonstrates social freedom. Using any materials you like, create the scene in layers so that when an individual looks through the hole in the box, he/she will see the depth of field in the scene. (See the illustration for an example.) When complete, place the lid on the box and view.

2. Banner

Using the patterns on the next two pages, create a banner that depicts social freedom. Use these symbols to create a border, enlarge the symbols to any desired large size, duplicate them in collage style, or trace them onto fabric and stitch them to a cloth banner. There are many possibilities. At the top of the banner add the words "Social Freedom."

3. Mosaic

Enlarge any of the following patterns to the desired size and create a mosaic by gluing down beads, painted seeds or beans, torn bits of paper, colored sand, or what-have-you.

4. Collage

Cut pictures from old magazines and other disposable printed materials that depict images of social freedom. You may also take photographs of such images, draw pictures yourself, or use the patterns on the following pages. Arrange these in a class collage under the header "Social Freedom."

Symbols of Freedom *(cont.)*

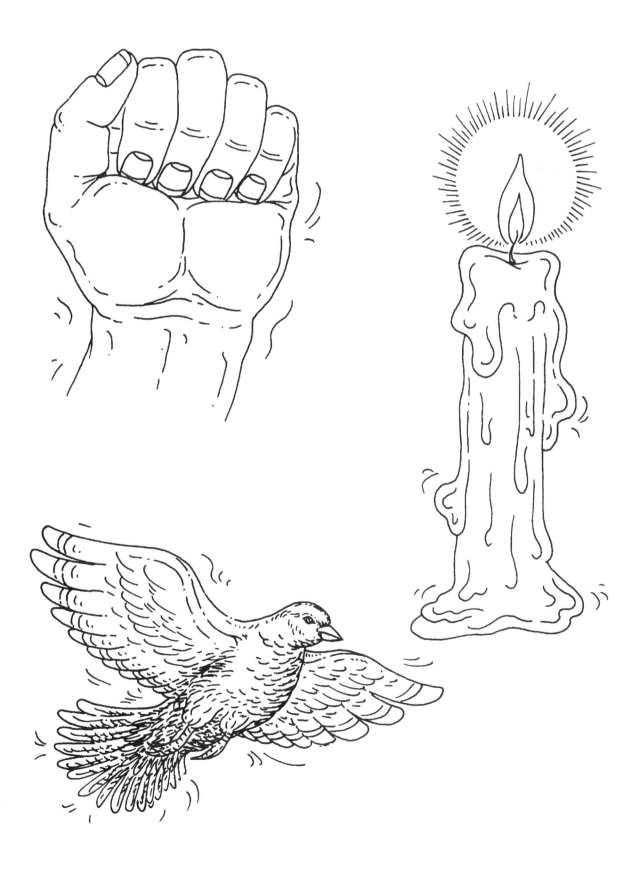

Symbols of Freedom *(cont.)*

Sounds From Around the World

Learning About Instruments

Many instruments that are unique to certain regions and countries have gained some international popularity in relatively recent years. These instruments create sounds that are often suggestive of the cultures from which they come, like the balalaika of Russia, the maracas of Brazil, and the sitar of India. Research these or other instruments that are generally foreign to your culture. Learn what they look like, how they are made, how they sound, and where they are used.

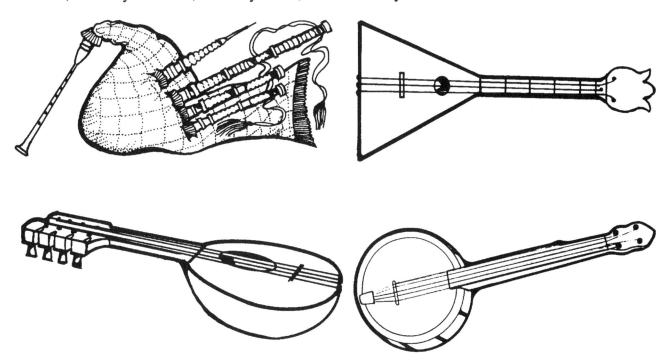

Making Maracas

Maracas are the simplest of these instruments to make. Technically, they are made of hollowed and dried gourds with pebbles or dried seeds placed inside. You can make one from these materials, or more simply, from a cardboard cylinder (such as an oatmeal canister) and unpopped popcorn. Once everyone has made a maraca or a pair of maracas, join in small groups to create a short piece of rhythm music. Practice and perform it for the class.

Listening to Other Sounds

Many modern artists have incorporated the distinct sounds of certain cultures into their popular music. Notable among these are Paul Simon who has utilized the sounds (as well as musicians) of South Africa and Gloria Estefan who incorporates Latin rhythms into much of her music. Research to find other artists who have done the same. As a class, listen to some of their work and discuss it. Can you trace the sounds and the instruments that might be playing them?

Challenge: From all you know about rock and roll, where do you think its sound originates? (There are many opinions about this, so no answer is the right answer. However, some responses can be better argued than others.)

Bread From Around the World

Bread is one of the few foods common to people all over the world. It is likely that in your country, some foreign breads are very popular. On the chart below, you will find the names of many kinds of breads and the countries from which they come. You will also find three simple recipes for some delicious breads from various parts of the world. Try them all and choose your favorite.

Country	Bread
Africa	sorghum bread
Austria	kugelhupf
China	almond cake
England	crumpet, English muffin
France	baguette, brioche, croissant
Germany	pretzel, pumpernickel
Greece	kouloura
Hungary	langos
India	chappatis
Ireland	soda bread
Israel	challah, matzah, pita
Italy	grissini, panettone
Japan	rice cake
Mexico	pan dulce, tortilla
Middle East	pita
Netherlands	doughnut
Russia	khachapuri, kulich
Scotland	bannock, scone
Sweden	flatbread
United States	cornbread, jonnycake, pizza (Italian origin)
Yugoslavia	poteca

Indian Chappatis

Ingredients:

- 1 ½ (370 mL) cups whole wheat flour
- ⅔ cup (170 mL) warm water
- ½ tsp. (3 mL) salt
- vegetable oil for cooking

Directions:

In a bowl, mix the flour and salt together; slowly stir in water until the dough forms into a ball. Knead dough on a lightly floured surface for 5-10 minutes, until smooth and sticky. Cover and let rise for 30 minutes. Cut the dough into 6 pieces and roll each into a flat circle with about an 8-inch (20 cm) diameter. Rub a frying pan with oil and heat until the oil smokes. Cook each flat circle of dough until brown and puffy on both sides. Serve immediately. Makes 6 chappatis.

Bread From Around the World *(cont.)*

German Pretzels (Soft)

Ingredients:

1 package active dry yeast

1 ½ cups (370 mL) warm water

1 tsp. (5 mL) salt

1 tsp. (5 mL) sugar

3 ½ to 4 cups (875 mL–1 L) all-purpose flour

(If using self-rising flour, omit salt.)

1 egg beaten

coarse salt

prepared mustard (optional)

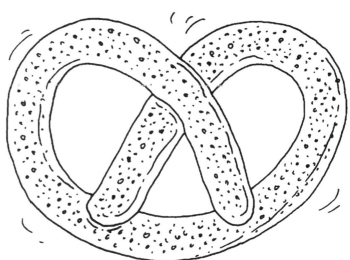

Directions:

Dissolve yeast in warm water in a large mixing bowl. Stir in salt, sugar, and 2 cups (500 mL) of flour. Beat until smooth. Stir in enough remaining flour to make dough easily manageable. Knead dough on a lightly floured surface until smooth and elastic (about 5 minutes). Place in greased bowl and turn greased sides up. Cover and let rise until double (about 45 to 60 minutes). Dough is ready if it does not spring back when touched. Heat oven to 425° F (218° C). Punch dough down and cut into 16 equal parts; roll each part into a rope about 18 inches (46 cm) long. Twist each rope into a pretzel shape, place on greased baking sheets, brush with beaten egg, and sprinkle with coarse salt. Bake until pretzels are brown, 15 to 20 minutes, and cool on wire rack. Makes 16 pretzels. Eat with mustard if desired.

American Pizza Bread

Ingredients:

1 tbsp. (15 mL) yellow cornmeal

2 cups (500 mL) all-purpose flour

2 tsps. (10 mL) baking powder

½ tsp. (2.5 mL) baking soda

¼ tsp. (1.3 mL) dried leaf basil, crushed

¼ tsp. (1.3 mL) dried leaf oregano, crushed

1 cup (250 mL) shredded provolone cheese

¾ cup (185 mL) grated Parmesan cheese

1 cup (250 mL) finely chopped pepperoni or salami

2 eggs at room temperature

1 8-oz. can (.24 L) tomato sauce

2 tbsps. (30 mL) olive or vegetable oil

⅛ tsp. (.6 mL) garlic powder or 1 medium garlic clove, minced

Directions:

Generously grease an 8-inch (20 cm) square baking pan. Sprinkle cornmeal over the bottom and set aside. Heat oven to 375°F (190°C) Combine flour, baking powder, baking soda, basil, and oregano in a large mixing bowl. Combine the two cheeses in a small bowl. Set aside one cup of the cheeses; add remaining cheese mixture and the chopped pepperoni or salami to the already mixed dry ingredients. In a medium bowl, beat eggs lightly; add tomato sauce, oil, and garlic. Add this to flour mixture, stirring only until moistened. Turn into baking pan and smooth; sprinkle with cup of cheese previously set aside. Place pepperoni slices on top and lightly press into the dough surface. Bake 35 to 40 minutes, until a wooden toothpick inserted in the center comes out clean. Let remain in pan to cool for 15 minutes; then cut into 9 to 16 pieces and serve hot or cold.

Name: _____ Date: _____

Soccer

Soccer is far and away the most popular sport around the world. It is the fastest growing amateur sport in the United States. To be a part of this international social pastime, it makes sense to know and understand the basic moves. Here they are. Practice them with your classmates and enjoy!

1. **Kicking:** Usually done with the instep. Stop the ball first, then kick it just over the ground.

2. **Dribbling:** Pass the ball back and forth between the feet, using the instep. Do this while running down the field.

4. **Tackling:** A player kicks or hooks the ball away from another player by using his/her feet, chest, or legs. In a sliding tackle, the player slides along the ground to hook the ball away. However it is done, the player tries not to make body contact with the individual he/she is tackling.

3. **Heading:** A player jumps up to meet the ball with his/her forehead. He/she snaps the forehead forward to strike the ball. Done properly, there is no harm to the head, though an incorrect hit can daze the player.

Name: _____ Date: _____

Trying Something New

In the 1992 Winter Olympics, the world was surprised by a bobsled team from Jamaica. What was so unusual is that Jamaica is a tropical country, and winter sports are virtually unheard of there. It was truly an amazing feat for the young people of Jamaica to develop an Olympic bobsledding team. You can learn all about this team and their wonderful spirit by watching the Disney film *Cool Runnings,* released in 1993.

Think about the countries listed below. For at least four of them, write down a sport that would be unusual for that country to participate in during the Olympic events, either summer or winter. You may wish first to brainstorm a list of as many Olympic sports as you can think of.

1. Australia _____

2. Canada _____

3. China _____

4. Egypt _____

5. India _____

6. Mexico _____

7. Russia _____

8. The United States _____

Share your ideas with the class and listen to the ideas of others.

Now, divide into small groups of three to four. Together, choose a sport that is not common or simple to perform in your area. Devise a plan for practicing this sport to prepare for Olympic competition. Write your plan here and on the back of this paper.

_____

_____

_____

_____

_____

_____

_____

_____

_____

The Education of Little Tree

by Forrest Carter (University of New Mexico Press, 1976)
(Available in UK, Random House UK; all others, UNM Press 505–277-2346)

Summary: When Little Tree's mother dies, the five-year-old is left orphaned. He finds a new home, however, with his grandparents, Wales and Bee, half and full-blood Cherokee. Thus begins *The Education of Little Tree.*

Wales and Bee are mountain people, and it is with them on the mountain that Little Tree uncovers the full range of his heritage and the fulfillment of his spirit. His story is told with the wonderful clarity that can come only from a child who is loved, nurtured, supported, and secure. Humor abounds in his story, and though it is balanced by poignancy and sadness, nothing told is artificial or contrived. The feelings are true and conveyed as such. Little Tree's point-of-view is untarnished and honest, and the reader cannot help but be captivated.

The warmth and love with which Little Tree is received by his grandparents is relayed to the reader with simple eloquence. We are there as Little Tree traverses the mountains with his grandpa, as he shares his secret place with his grandma, as he fishes, and frolics, and leads the childhood about which many people simply dream. It is ironic then, that the outside world chooses to blind itself to the true experiences of Little Tree and instead judges his experience and caretaking by its own predetermined standards. The Law is used to remove the boy from his home. He is placed in a Christian orphanage, and from before the time he enters the door, he is branded as evil, a savage, and a bastard (his parents were married by the Cherokee and not by the government).

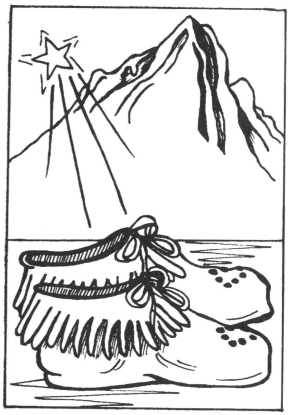

This, however, is not the end of Little Tree, nor is it the end of his time with his grandparents. They are reunited triumphantly, and Little Tree's education continues. So, it might be added, does the reader's.

Throughout the novel, the reader is made privy to the "Way of the Cherokee." We see first-hand the richness of life, both in solemnity and celebration. The Way is unfamiliar to many, but its truth—its alignment with right order, harmony, and nature—cannot be denied. We cannot help but praise and admire the worth of Little Tree's experiences.

It is for this reason that *The Education of Little Tree* is the ideal novel to read in order to learn about social freedom. It depicts a pattern for living that is little followed and less understood, but its value and beauty are so admirable that the reader will likely wish to discover more. It is truly a lovely novel, beautifully written and earnestly read.

Name: _____ Date: _____

"I Kin Ye"

Simple and direct language is clearly important to Little Tree and his grandparents. No unnecessary word is spoken, and anything that is said is stated exactly as it is meant. Of course, one must know the language first in order to understand its dialectic subtleties, and herein lies one of the charms of Little Tree. The dialect, peculiar to the region and the Cherokee, is so filled with warmth, character, and artistry that the reader is completely captivated.

Choose any three chapters from *The Education of Little Tree.* From these, find at least ten words and phrases that are peculiar to the dialect of the book. Next to each, write your own definition or explanation of its meaning. Share them with the class.

Chapter	Dialect Word/Phrase	Definition/Explanation
_____	_____	_____
_____	_____	_____
_____	_____	_____
_____	_____	_____
_____	_____	_____
_____	_____	_____
_____	_____	_____
_____	_____	_____
_____	_____	_____
_____	_____	_____
_____	_____	_____
_____	_____	_____

Name: _____ Date: _____

Remembrances

Clearly, there is a great deal of love between Little Tree, his grandparents, and special friends like Willow John and Mr. Wine. There are ties of heart and spirit that keep them connected, even when physically separated. When Little Tree is in the orphanage, he and those dear to him arrange to look at the Dog Star every evening and send "remembrances" to one another. Little Tree is comforted by the loving images that come to his mind, quite sure that they are sent to him by those missing him back home. He sends thoughtful remembrances to them as well.

If you were separated from those you love and who love you, what remembrances would you send? Choose one or two special people in your life, write their names below, and after each write two or three significant remembrances that are meaningful to both you and the other person.

_____
(name)

_____

_____

_____

_____

_____

_____
(name)

_____

_____

_____

_____

Name: _____ Date: _____

"Next Time Will Be Better..."

In reading about cultures other than your own, you will come to find that people around the world hold many different beliefs. Though individuals are basically the same in their need for food, clothing, and shelter, as well as their emotional need for love, acceptance, understanding, and companionship, how they go about living and what they believe about life and themselves can vary tremendously.

One of the most striking instances of this in *The Education of Little Tree* is the whole experience of death and the after-life. A careful reader will notice that when Bee, Wales, and Willow John each die, there is both an element of choice in their deaths and a belief that this time on earth is not their last. Though when Mr. Wine dies, the reader is not sure whether he has chosen death at this time or is simply aware that the time has come, his meticulous preparations for death suggest one or the other.

There is mention, too, of the spirits of each person. After death, those who are living still can see the spirit move in the wind, shaking the leaves on the trees and disturbing birds in flight. There is nothing frightening about this to the living. Rather, they rejoice in the "free spirit" of the newly departed. Even Little Tree's dog, in the final sequence of the book, is said to have this same thriving, ongoing spirit.

For your assignment, you may do one of two things:

1. Write your own beliefs about death and the afterlife. Give as much information and detail as possible, being true to what you actually do believe.

2. Research the beliefs of a culture other than your own, and in detail describe those beliefs in a way to make them understandable for the class. Share what you have learned with the class.

   Respond below and on the back of this page.

_____

_____

_____

_____

_____

_____

_____

_____

_____

_____

_____

_____

_____

Name: _____ Date: _____

The Cherokee Nation

In the early part of the 1800's, white settlers in the United States demanded that the government relocate all Indians living in the Southeast to land west of the Mississippi. A treaty was signed in 1835, in which some Cherokee agreed to move. Most others, led by Chief John Ross, did not. In the winter of 1838-1839, the remaining Cherokee were forced to leave their homeland and walk to Oklahoma in what is now called The Trail of Tears. Though approximately 1,000 people were able to escape to the Smoky Mountains, thousands of the other Cherokee died along the way to Oklahoma. Walking conditions were hard, of course, but many say that the discouragement bred over years was far worse on the nation of people and is the primary cause for so many deaths. In true Cherokee spirit, however, those who made it to Oklahoma established the new Cherokee Nation there.

The Trail of Tears

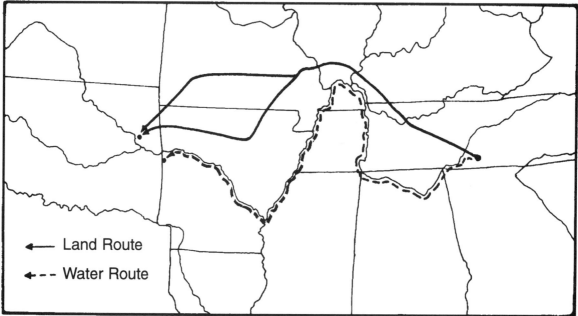

◄——— Land Route

◄- - - Water Route

As had become its pattern, the United States government stepped in at this point to abolish the Nation. The land given to the Cherokee was reopened for white settlement. This is what Willow John learned when he travelled to the Nation. Yet, despite this action on the part of the government, the Cherokee spirit has prevailed. Tribal government has been reestablished in northeastern Oklahoma, and the Cherokee Nation is ever growing in strength, financial security, and cultural richness. It is thought of as the second most influential Native American power in the United States, and it stands strong under intelligent leadership.

Sometimes in reading about historic events, it is easy to ignore the emotional reality behind them due to the distance created by time. To better understand the experience of the Cherokee, imagine that you, your family, and your entire community are forced to gather only those things you can carry and walk hundreds of miles to a land completely unfamiliar to you. In fact, the land to which you are relocated is as different from your current surroundings as night is to day. The homes you are leaving are being sold to incoming settlers from another part of the country. You will receive no payment for your lost homes.

American Indians

Following is a partial listing of Indian tribes (and tribal groupings) from North, Central, and South America. Choose one tribe and do research on it to find out about its customary *clothing, shelter, food, games/entertainment, work, family life,* and *beliefs.* Be prepared to present the information you learn to the class.

Algonquin	Chinook	Klamath	Pawnee
Apache	Chippewa	Kwakiutl	Pima
Arapaho	Choctaw	Mahican	Powhatan
Araucanian	Chumash	Maya	Seminole
Arawak	Comanche	Mohave	Shoshone
Aztec	Cree	Natchez	Sioux
Beaver	Crow	Navajo	Taos
Blackfeet	Hopi	Nez Perce	Tarascan
Carib	Inca	Nootka	Toltec
Cherokee (Little	Iroquois	Olmec	Wichita
Tree's ancestry)	Jivaro	Omaha	Yanomami
Cheyenne	Kickapoo	Osage	Zapotec
Chibcha	Kiowa	Paiute	Zuni

The following chart may help you organize the notes for your research.

Tribe: _____

1. Clothing:

2. Shelter:

3. Food:

4. Games/Entertainment:

5. Work:

6. Family Life:

7. Beliefs:

Name: _____ Date: _____

Judaism

Judaism is introduced in *The Education of Little Tree* through the character of Mr. Wine. Find definitions or descriptions for each of the following terms that relate to Judaism. If you are Jewish, they will likely be familiar to you. If you are not, then think about similar customs, things, and people in your religious or cultural tradition. (**Note:** Both Christianity and Islam originated in Judaism.)

Terms	Definition or Description
1. Hebrews	
2. Rabbi	
3. Talmud	
4. Torah	
5. Siddur	
6. Abraham	
7. Sarah	
8. Isaac	
9. Rebecca	
10. Jacob (Israel)	
11. Leah	
12. Rachel	
13. Rosh Hashanah	
14. Yom Kippur	
15. Passover	
16. Shavuot	
17. Sukkot	
18. Hanukkah	
19. The Ten Commandments	
20. Synagogue	
21. Sabbath	
22. Yarmulka	
23. Exodus	
24. Judah/Judea	
25. Canaan	

Name: _____ Date: _____

Weddings

Virtually every culture has a traditional ceremony for the beginning of a marriage. These ceremonies and their customs are often firmly planted in cultural tradition and can date back many hundreds of years. For example, western tradition suggests that the new bride will throw her bouquet of flowers to the unmarried females in attendance. It is said that the one to catch the bouquet will be the next to marry. This tradition likely stems back to France 700 years ago.

What traditions are part of your cultural heritage? Brainstorm for all those you know in the space below.

_____

_____

_____

_____

_____

_____

_____

_____

_____

_____

_____

_____

- Share the ideas above with the rest of the class. Explain any customs you know that your classmates do not.

- Now, as a class, do some research to discover the traditional Cherokee wedding ceremony and customs. If someone in your class is of Cherokee descent, you may already have found out!

Name: _____ Date: _____

Light

A common symbol for freedom is light. Often when protesters are rallying for a certain cause, they will hold single candles, symbolizing the need for enlightenment. It is their wish that the minds of society will open up to receive their cause, and that all people will join together in support of it.

In *The Education of Little Tree,* light is also a vehicle for enlightenment and union. Mr. Wine lights a candle, just as his family across the world does, to join with them symbolically and spiritually, though they are geographically separated. Little Tree and his loved ones look at the brilliant Dog Star (Sirius) to do the same thing. And as Little Tree and Wales watch the beautiful mountain sunrise shed a glow like fire across the landscape, Wales is moved to declare, "She's coming alive!" He and Little Tree know the beauty and wonder of the land, and they wish others of the world would join them in knowing the same. For them, life and light go hand in hand.

If you had the opportunity to join with the world to share a message of enlightenment, what would it be? What do you think is something the world needs to know in order to be drawn together for the good of everyone and the planet? Across the image of light illustrated below, write your message clearly and simply, just as Little Tree would.

Reader's Response

To do a Reader's Response, you will need several sheets of paper. Either draw a vertical line down the middle of each or use a stenographer's notepad. At the top of the left-hand side write, "Characters and Quotes," and at the top of the right-hand side write, "Response."

As you read a chapter in the novel, write the chapter number or title in the far left-hand margin. Next to it, write any quotation or character reference that strikes you. In other words, write down anything that makes you have an internal response or starts you thinking. Then, in the right-hand column, write your response to the quote. Examples are included to start you on your way.

Chapter	Characters and Quotes	Response
Chapter 1	". . . the bus driver turned around to the crowd in the bus and lifted his right hand and said, *'How!'* and laughed, and all the people laughed."	I feel really angry about this, angry at the ignorance and rudeness of the people on the bus.
	"I felt better about it, knowing they was friendly and didn't take offense because we didn't have a ticket."	It's amazing how much better I feel just because Little Tree saw everything this way. He seems so innocent.
	"She was unnatural black all around her eyes and her mouth was red all over from blood."	This is really funny. He thinks she is sick because of her make-up. That says a lot about make-up, I think!
	". . . whispers and sighs began to feather through the trees . . ."	That is a pretty image. I can see it and feel it.
	"I knew I was Little Tree, and I was happy that they loved me and wanted me."	I'm glad he feels so secure with his grandparents. Their house seems like a good place for him to be.

To the teacher: Later, students can choose one of their responses and extend their ideas into an essay or story.

Personal Freedom

The Unrestricted Space and Leisure to Know Oneself

Name: _____ Date: _____

"I Am" Poem

Complete the poem frame below, choosing words and phrases that tell about you. You can choose your own way of responding. The poem itself is free verse; it does not need to rhyme. The last line in each verse should repeat the first.

I am _____ .

I wonder _____ .

I hear _____ .

I see _____ .

I want _____ .

I am _____ .

I pretend _____ .

I feel _____ .

I touch _____ .

I worry _____ .

I cry _____ .

I am _____ .

I understand _____ .

I say _____ .

I dream _____ .

I try _____ .

I hope _____ .

I am _____ .

"Me" Vocabulary

If you were to draw a picture of someone, you would probably use a pen or pencil, crayons or paint. But can a painting or drawing show what someone's personality is? Can it show what a person feels and how that person thinks?

This activity asks you to "draw" a picture of yourself with words, ones that "paint" a picture of what you are like inside. The words are meant to be symbolic; therefore, they will be representations of you.

When you have completed this activity, you can take the words a step further by doing the project described on the following page. (**Note to the teacher:** see page 145.)

Choose words from the following categories.

Categories:	Examples:
15 SIGHT words	sparkling, luminous, freckled
15 TASTE words	salty, sweet, bitter
15 TOUCH words	bristly, fragile, silky
15 SMELL words	fragrant, musty, perfumed
15 SOUND words	squeaky, buzzing, strumming
10 ACTIONS	climbing, thinking, swimming
10 OBJECTS	merry-go-round, ice cream cone, sunflower
5 ABSTRACTIONS	freedom, serenity, enthusiasm

As you can see, your word choices should be specific. For example, as an abstraction, *love* is general, but *friendship, romance,* or *captivation* are more specific.

	Sight	Taste	Touch	Smell	Sound	Action	Object	Abstraction
1.								
2.								
3.								
4.								
5.								
6.								
7.								
8.								
9.								
10.								
11.								
12.								
13.								
14.								
15.								

Name: _____ Date: _____

Creating a Character

Before writing a story, it is a good idea for an author to first think about the characters that will be portrayed. Naming them is important, of course, but even more important is considering the kind of people they are, what they like, what they think, and so forth. Filling in a sheet like the one below for each of the primary characters may help.

Do some thinking about a character who appeals to you. Then fill out this sheet, making up the statistics and characteristics as you go. Remember, this character can be anything you want!

Challenge: When you have completed the form, create a story for the character.

Character's Full Name:_____ Height: _____ Weight: _____

Birth Date: _____ Current Age:_____ Hair Color: _____ Eye Color:_____

Place of Birth:_____ Distinguishing Features:_____

Residence: _____

Occupation: _____

Ethnic Background:_____

Style of Dress: _____

Parents' Names/Vital Information: _____

Siblings' Names/Vital Information (if applicable):_____

Spouse's Name/Vital Information (if applicable): _____

Child(ren)'s Name(s)/Vital Information (if applicable): _____

Pets: _____

Hobbies:_____

Favorite

    Place: _____

    Possession:_____

    Food: _____

    Color: _____

    Publication: _____

    Person/Celebrity: _____

    Movie/Television Show: _____

Fears: _____

Dreams for the Future: _____

Where Most Days Are Spent: _____

Where Most Nights Are Spent: _____

Debate

Public Education

Many nations provide free and public education for all children. It is a right, guaranteed under law. Everyone must be offered the opportunity for education, and in many places, that opportunity must be accepted. However, not every school is able to offer circumstances that support the education of all students in a safe and nurturing atmosphere. In urban areas in particular (though not exclusive to them), crime, disrespect, racial tension, and school drop-out rates are on the rise. Given that, is the educational opportunity offered to all really equal? Is opportunity there when peace and safety are not?

☞ Where do you stand? Think about it; then turn to the next page.

Gun Control

In those nations where individuals have the free opportunity to own guns, the rate of violent crimes committed using those guns is often higher than nations where guns are prohibited. Yet many individuals argue that should guns become prohibited, criminals will still have possession of them, whereas honest citizens will be without protection. The United States' government provides for the right to own and bear arms in its Bill of Rights. Because there are strong arguments on both sides of the issue, the debate over gun control is ever-increasing.

☞ Where do you stand? Think about it; then turn to the next page.

Prayer in School

In some countries, prayer is a common component of the school day, particularly in religious schools. Students in a classroom or in the whole school will gather for silent prayer or a common one spoken aloud. In other countries, formalized prayer or a formal prayer time in school is forbidden. There are those who argue that a decline in world harmony can be directly linked to a decline in prayer. Others strongly urge that prayer is always a matter of personal choice and should never be urged publicly, but only on a personal scale.

☞ Where do you stand? Think about it; then turn to the next page.

Debate *(cont.)*

A **debate** is argumentation both for and against a proposition. It is oral and the language is formal. The **proposition** is a precise statement worded in the affirmative. It makes clear both the affirmative and negative positions.

Choose the topic on the previous page that interests you most. Meet with others in the class who have also chosen your topic. Together, follow the steps below for preparing and holding a classroom debate. (These or other topics might also be debated at a schoolwide event.)

1. **Word your proposition.** Follow these guidelines:

    a. State it in the affirmative. The statement and its two sides will then be clear.

    b. Choose simple and specific words so that no one argues the meaning of the words themselves instead of the proposition as a whole.

    c. Begin the proposition, "Resolved . . ." (For example, "Resolved, that five minutes should be set aside at the start of every school day for silent prayer."

2. **Choose your side of the argument and join with others on your side.** Ideally, the two sides will have an equal number of people.

3. **Together with the members of your group (side), prepare your arguments.** Remember to stick to the proposition.

    a. Research to find supportive data.

    b. Talk to experts.

    c. Organize your arguments logically and clearly.

    d. Challenge one another by finding the weak points in your arguments and responding to them.

4. **Hold the debate.**

    a. Choose a judge or group of judges. After the debate, the judge(s) will decide whether the proposition passes or fails.

    b. While debating, keep to the proposition. Do not argue other points or the semantics of the proposition.

    c. State your case. The standard format for a formal debate is as follows:

    - The affirmative speaks for ten minutes. This is called a *constructive speech.* The negative listens to the arguments of the affirmative.
    - The negative speaks for ten minutes while the affirmative listens.
    - The affirmative speaks a second constructive speech for ten minutes.
    - The negative speaks a second constructive speech for ten minutes.
    - The affirmative gives a *rebuttal speech.* A rebuttal is a direct response to the arguments of the other side. There are five minutes to rebut.
    - The negative rebuts the arguments of the affirmative, also in five minutes.
    - The affirmative gives a second rebuttal. Again, there are five minutes.
    - The negative gives a second rebuttal, also in five minutes.
    - The judges determine whether the proposition passes or fails. They do so by casting votes.

Name: _____ Date: _____

Values

Everyone has a set of values by which he or she lives. Values are those ideas and behaviors that are most important to an individual. People learn about values from their parents, caretakers, friends, and peers. Sometimes an individual's values closely match those of the people around him/her, but sometimes they simply reflect the values of others or are entirely dissimilar. The reason for this is that everyone is unique. No two people will have exactly the same values, just as no two people will have exactly the same fingerprints.

Complete the chart below, checking off the appropriate place on the value scale that matches your feelings about the item. There are no right and wrong answers. Just be true to yourself.

(1 = highly valued; 2 = valued; 3 = somewhat valued; 4 = little valued; 5 = not valued)

Item	Value Scale				
	1	**2**	**3**	**4**	**5**
Winning games					
Being athletic					
Getting good grades					
Completing jobs or projects					
Having my parents' respect					
Being liked by my teacher					
Being funny					
Looking good					
Dressing well					
Having my own bike/transportation					
Having a pet					
Being with my family					
Being neat					
Being honest					
Having money of my own					
Being appreciated					
Being alone					
Being with friends					
Being popular					
Having a best friend					
Having a boyfriend/girlfriend					
Travelling					
Going to a good school					
Celebrating holidays					
Having a hobby					

Name: _____ Date: _____

Self-Esteem

Complete the following sentences. There are no right and wrong answers. Just be true to yourself.

1. I am _____ .

2. When I am 30, I expect to be _____ .

3. Love is _____ .

4. Most people think of me as _____ .

5. I am proud of myself when _____ .

6. People my age need _____ .

7. Very young children need _____ .

8. It is normal human nature to _____ .

9. My father is _____ .

10. My mother is _____ .

11. A good teacher is one who _____ .

12. One of the best things about me is _____ .

13. Something that seems unfair is _____ .

14. When I am criticized by others, I _____ .

15. When I am angry, I _____ .

16. Brothers and sisters are _____ .

17. It is no use to _____ .

18. One of my favorite things to do is _____ .

19. My best friend is _____ .

20. When I make a mistake, I _____ .

21. At home, we _____ .

22. In choosing my career, the most important thing is _____ .

23. I am happiest when _____ .

24. One of my favorite places is _____ .

25. The characteristics of people I most like to be around are _____ .

Planning a Budget

Every self-supporting adult must plan a budget in order to avoid financial difficulties. A budget is a plan for expected costs over a set period of time, as well as preparation for unexpected costs.

Here are some standard expenses:

- Rent/Mortgage
- Utilities (electric, gas, phone, water, etc.)
- Groceries
- Health Care/Insurance
- Clothing
- Entertainment
- Auto (gas, insurance, upkeep, parking) or Other Transportation (cab/subway fare)
- Savings Account Deposit

Some people have additional monthly expenses, depending on their lifestyles or circumstances. These include (but are not limited to):

- Loan/Credit Payments
- Payments for Services Rendered (gardening, cleaning, babysitting, etc.)
- Childcare
- Child/Spousal Support Payments
- Charitable Donations

To begin planning a budget, determine your expected income. Divide the total amount according to your expenses. Consider how much is appropriate and reasonable to spend on each necessity, as well as how much you would like to set aside for amounts which can fluctuate, such as entertainment and clothing.

In order to practice with budgets, work with a net monthly income of $1,100. (This is roughly the net income for an individual earning $20,000 per year, after taxes.)

- Research to determine the costs of the items listed above.
- Plan out the monthly expenses.
- Is this income feasible?
- Is more income necessary?
- Is there any way to trim the budget?

Options:

1. Plan a budget for the character you created on page 138.

2. Determine a career that you are interested in pursuing and research to find that career's average income in your area. Plan a budget accordingly.

Name: _____ Date: _____

Scientific Characterizations

A true scientist uses the power of observation to help characterize and classify any object, phenomena, or being. Scientific description is meticulous, careful to note every detail in addition to the obvious.

In characterizing anything, a scientist will objectify it and break it down into its component parts. For example, a tree will be considered by its leaves, branches, trunk, roots, and so forth. It will also likely be considered in regards to its environment and how it acts and reacts in it. Scientists think things through from every possible angle.

Now is your opportunity to do the same. Choose any living thing: plant, animal, or human being. Think about it as a whole as well as a collection of parts. For example, if you choose a specific dog, consider its overall nature, and then take note of its eyes (color, shape, vision), ears (size, shape, hearing), fur (color, texture), bark (pitch) age, weight, etc. Pay attention to its environment, also. See how detailed you can be, and note everything in written form, clearly and in an organized manner. When complete, you should have a thorough written portrait of your "specimen."

Begin your characterization here and continue on the back. You may use more paper as well. Some ideas are given below to get you started.

Plants	Animals	Humans
Roots	Legs	Eyes
Leaves	Fur/skin	Ears
Blossoms	Ears	Nose
Stems	Nose	Skin
Color	Weight	Weight
Height	Height	Height

_____
(living thing)

_____

_____

_____

_____

_____

"Me" Vocabulary, Part 2

First do the activity on page 137. Once you have all 100 words that describe and characterize you, then you can begin this part of the project.

Materials:

They are up to you.

Directions:

You will decide that, too.

You see, this project is meant to convey, in some symbolic form, who you are and how you perceive yourself. You will need to decide upon an object or image that suits you. For example, if you think of yourself as lovable and huggable, you might be a teddy bear. If you think of yourself as bright and shining, you might be a star. If you are active you might be a top, and if quick you might be a cheetah. When you decide upon the right object, you will know it because it will "click" for you inside.

Once you have determined your object, you will then need to figure a way to present your words and object together. The words might form the lines of the object as it is drawn. Or the object can be molded out of clay with the words carved into it. You might also choose to do a painting where the words are drawn in picture form together with the object. (In that case, you will also need to provide the word list.) There are so many more possibilities, too. Go as far as your imagination will let you. Be creative and open-minded. This is your opportunity to say who you are!

Name: _____ Date: _____

Who I Am Inside

Close your eyes for a minute. With your inner vision, look inside yourself. How do you feel? What do you think? Who do you say that you are? Consider all of these questions for a few minutes. Try to block out what you think others think of you or what they have told you about yourself. Think about only what you know.

Now, open your eyes and write your thoughts here.

_____

_____

_____

_____

_____

_____

_____

_____

_____

_____

_____

_____

_____

_____

_____

_____

_____

_____

_____

_____

Look over what you just wrote. Does it suggest anything to you?

Here is your assignment. Without using words, figure out a visual way to share this information about you with someone else. This can be a drawing, sculpture, collage, or truly any other art form or medium that expresses what you want. Just be sure it "tells" the truth of who you are as you see it.

Name: _____ Date: _____

Mandala

A *mandala* is a visual representation of who you are in symbolic form. It shows both the outer you (sun sign) and the inner you (moon signs). You can choose the items that go in the mandala by filling in a chart like the one given below. The **sun sign** is the specific item that represents you under the given category. For example, the animal sun sign, if you are a playful, happy person, might be a puppy. The **characteristic** it has that you also have is "playfulness." The **opposite characteristic** is whatever you perceive to be the opposite of the characteristic just given. In this case it might be "seriousness." The **moon sign** is the specific item under the category that has the "opposite characteristic" just given. A spider may be chosen as a "serious animal."

Fill in the chart below according to the direction given above. Everything you fill in should apply to you.

	Sun Sign	Characteristic	Opposite Characteristic	Moon Sign
Animal				
Plant				
Gem/Mineral				
Weather/Season				
Color				
Number				

Now turn to the next page.

Name: _____ Date: _____

Mandala *(cont.)*

In the mandala below, draw and color the things from your chart on the previous page. Fill in the sun signs on the left and the moon signs on the right.

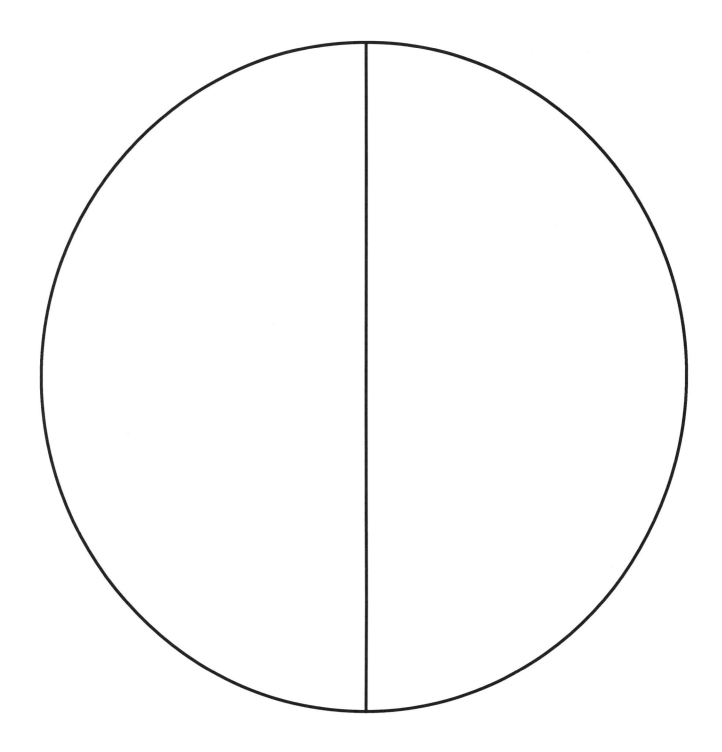

Name: _____ Date: _____

My Instrument

Every instrument ever invented has its own, distinctive sound. A cello's rich notes are nothing like the light breeziness of the flute or rhythmic tones of the drums. Each is unique, and in that uniqueness, very special. So, too, is every human being. The people around you are like you in only the most superficial of ways. Human beings are far too complex to be replicated in another person. Their individual "sound" is very distinct.

What is your sound? In order to determine that, the first thing to do is to brainstorm for all the instruments you know. Write them here.

_____   _____

_____   _____

_____   _____

_____   _____

_____   _____

Look at the list above. Circle or highlight any that you think apply to you. Now look at them again. Which of the instruments you circled or highlighted is most like you? Write your choice below, as well as your explanation of why that instrument is a good representative for you.

_____
my choice

_____

_____

_____

_____

_____

Challenge: Find a piece of music from the instrument of your choice that you feel "sounds" like you. Bring the music in to share with your class, explaining the connection between you and the music.

Name: _____ Date: _____

Your Integrity

If anything will get a person through in life, it is *integrity.* Integrity is what an individual has when he or she remains true to his or her values. Literally, integrity is a state of *wholeness* or *completeness,* so a person with integrity is whole and complete within him/herself.

Here is a fun and interesting way to discover your own true sense of integrity.

1. List the names of five to ten people whom you admire. Next to each name, write two to three admirable characteristics of that person.

   _____   _____

   _____   _____

   _____   _____

   _____   _____

   _____   _____

2. List here each of the characteristics named above. Tally next to each characteristic how many times you mentioned it.

   _____   _____

   _____   _____

   _____   _____

   _____   _____

   _____   _____

3. Put the characteristics in order according to the tally.

   _____   _____

   _____   _____

   _____   _____

   _____   _____

   _____   _____

These characteristics make up your own personal integrity. You admire them in others, and you only feel whole and complete when you reflect them in yourself.

Name: _____ Date: _____

What Is Your Talent?

There are some people who are naturally and obviously gifted athletes. They excel, just as those with a true musical, artistic, or mathematical gift excel. Yet, there are many more who have some degree of athletic talent, though they may not shine like the stars. Their talents usually fall in specific areas, and are often supplemented by strong character traits. Here are just a few of these talents and traits:

- Running
- Jumping
- Climbing
- Aiming
- Catching
- Throwing
- Shooting
- Poise
- Stamina
- Perseverance
- Determination

- _____
- _____
- _____
- _____
- _____
- _____
- _____
- _____
- _____
- _____
- _____

Look over the list above. Together with the class, brainstorm for additional physical talents and character traits and add them to the list.

Now answer the following questions.

1. From the list given above, where do you think your talent lies?

   _____

   _____

   _____

   _____

2. Given that talent, what sport do you think best suits you?

   _____

   _____

   _____

   _____

Challenge: If everyone in the class finds another student who has a similar talent, then as a class, you can host a competition that pits those talents against each other.

The Secret Garden

by Francis Hodgson Burnett (Yearling Classics, 1989; originally published 1911)

(Available in Canada, Dell; UK, Armada Bks; Australia, Transworld Publishers)

Summary: Born to wealthy, elegant, and emotionally uninvolved parents, Mary Lennox spends her first ten years of life as a virtual orphan in India. The only contact she has is with her *Ayah* (nurse) and other servants of the house. They treat the little British girl as royalty. She does nothing for herself. They even dress her as though she were a doll. She is unloved, and because of this, she becomes as hard and unfeeling as stone.

When tragedy strikes and Mary's parents, Ayah, and many other servants of the house die quickly of cholera, Mary is completely forgotten by all. Outsiders assume that she, too, has died. However, she is found quite by chance when colleagues of her father look over what they think is her family's abandoned house.

Mary's legal guardian is her uncle, Archibald Craven, whom she has never met. He lives in Misselthwaite Manor, a large and rambling home on the English moors, and Mary is sent there to live with him. She is met at the docks by his senior housekeeper, Mrs. Medlock, a harsh woman who has no desire to care for the odd, peaked, young girl. They travel for miles to the manor, where Mary is shown her room (which is not at all designed for a child) and told to keep very close to quarters. She is not introduced to her uncle, but instead meets only servants. She expects them to care for her as the Indian servants did, but they, of course, do not. A young servant girl of Yorkshire heritage, Martha Sowerby, helps Mary make the transition to self-sufficiency. She learns to dress herself, and at Martha's encouragement, begins to spend time out-of-doors, running and jumping rope. She also learns from Martha and a gardener, Ben Weatherstaff, of the existence of a secret garden, which has been kept locked and unattended since the death of Mary's aunt ten years earlier. It seems she fell from a tree there, and Mr. Craven, who loved her very much, ordered the key to the garden buried. He fell into a mourning that has not ceased in all the years since.

Through the help of a robin which has taken a liking to Mary, she uncovers the garden as well as the key. Martha's brother, Dickon, a twelve-year-old who is said to charm wild animals and roam the moor, at one with nature, helps Mary to revive the garden to all its splendor. Mary eventually meets her uncle, who unwittingly offers her the garden for her own keeping. More surprisingly, Mary learns of the existence of her ten-year-old cousin, Colin, who is kept as an invalid on the other side of the house. Together, Mary, Dickon, and the garden revive Colin, just as she herself revives through the glory of nature and friendship. Colin grows strong, Mary friendly, and Mr. Craven begins to leave his mourning behind, renewing his relationship with his son. Not only has the concealed garden begun to flourish as a garden should, but it has made the "secret garden" of their souls begin to grow with color, life, and energy.

152

Name: _____ Date: _____

"Mistress Mary, Quite Contrary"

When Mary first leaves the home of her parents, she stays briefly with the local minister and his family. There, she is so contrary and unlike the other children, that they quickly dub her "Mistress Mary" after the nursery rhyme. They chant:

> *Mistress Mary, quite contrary,*
> *How does your garden grow?*
> *With silver bells, and cockle shells,*
> *And marigolds all in a row.*

The minster's wife hears the rhyme and thinks it unfeeling, but she also cannot help but see the truth in it. The little girl is contrary, as contrary as she can be.

Together with your class, brainstorm for all the nursery rhymes and songs you know, from "Baa, Baa, Black Sheep" to "Wee Willie Winkie." Look them over and think about their words and meanings.

Now, think about yourself. Which nursery rhyme seems to suit *you* best? It may not reflect who you are all the time, but rather who you are some of the time, or even how you sometimes feel inside. Write the nursery rhyme you have chosen on the lines below. On the back of this paper write about the connection you found between you and the nursery rhyme.

Name: _____ Date: _____

The Garden

The garden that Mary uncovers is at first gray and quiet, but the hope of life runs through the withering vines. She knows it is truly a beautiful, wild, and growing thing. As she tends to it, it blossoms into vibrant, tangled color. It is full of life, joy, and energy, just as Mary is as the novel progresses. At times it seems that Mary and the garden are one and the same.

If there was a garden that stood for you, that reflected who you are inside, what would it look like? What would grow there? How would things be arranged? Would it be enclosed or open? Is it quiet or lively? Are others happy to visit? Is wildlife safe and comfortable there? Think about these things.

Now, draw or write about your garden here. Remember, this garden represents who you are. Be prepared to explain how it is like you.

Name: _____ Date: _____

The Characters

There are many characters in *The Secret Garden,* fitting many personality types. After the name of each character given below, briefly describe his or her personality.

Character	Personality Description
1. Mary Lennox	
2. Martha Sowerby	
3. Mrs. Medlock	
4. Dickon Sowerby	
5. Colin Craven	
6. Archibald Craven	
7. Susan Sowerby	
8. Mem Sahib	

Respond:

1. Which of these characters is most like you?

   _____

   _____

   _____

2. Why?

   _____

   _____

   _____

Name: _____ Date: _____

Flowers

As is natural, there are many flowers and plants mentioned in this novel, each unique and beautiful in its own way. Listed below are some of the most frequently mentioned ones. Look up each flower in the encyclopedia or other reference books, and write a brief description of it here. Then answer the questions at the bottom of the page.

1. Broom	
2. Crocus	
3. Daffodil	
4. Gorse	
5. Heather	
6. Lily of the Valley	
7. Marigold	
8. Narcissus	
9. Rose	
10. Snapdragon	
11. Snowdrop	
12. Thistle	

Respond:

1. If you were one of these flowers, which would you be? (Or, is there a flower that is not mentioned that suits you better?)

   _____

   _____

   _____

2. Why and how are you like this flower?

   _____

   _____

   _____

Name: _____ Date: _____

Mary Lennox

Mary Lennox is a particularly interesting character. She unfolds before the reader as the novel progresses. Initially, she is spoiled, demanding, unloved, and unlovable. Her contrary attitude is ever evident. Yet, the reader knows that she has been abandoned emotionally by her parents, and that she is ultimately forgotten by everyone around her. Surely her manner has grown from this, and possibly there is another kind of child waiting beneath the surface. When Mary moves to Misselthwaite, the reader begins to see that this is so. The moor air, the garden, and the friendships of Martha, Dickon, Ben Weatherstaff, Colin, and the robin begin to bring forth the true little girl, until she is fully developed and free at the novel's end.

Using the novel as a guide, find what each of the following characters thinks of Mary when he/she first meets the girl and then, again, at the end of the novel.

What They Think of Mary

Characters	At the First Meeting	At the End
Mrs. Medlock		
Martha		
Ben		
Mary Herself		

Name: _____ Date: _____

What Would Be Written About You?

When characters are presented in a novel, the reader finds out about them in three different ways: (1) what the author says about them, (2) what other characters say about them, and (3) what they say about themselves. If you were a character in a novel, what would be written about you? Respond to each of the questions below.

1. What would the author write about you?

   _____
   _____
   _____
   _____
   _____

2. What would another character say/think about you? (Name and describe your relationship to this other character.)

   _____
   _____
   _____
   _____
   _____

3. What would you say about yourself?

   _____
   _____
   _____
   _____
   _____

Name: _____ Date: _____

Birds

Birds are a traditional symbol for freedom. Their ability to fly is enviable to the land-bound human being, for birds carry within them the means to absolute liberty. We have searched for centuries to discover a way to copy their freedom of movement and make it our own, and, of course, in recent history we have experienced some success. Even so, the innate ability of birds is beyond us, and we can only yearn to "try our wings" as the birds do.

In a very real way, the little robin of *The Secret Garden* offers Mary the key to her personal freedom. In showing her the key to the garden and the garden door, the robin gives Mary the means to uncover her true self and the vitality within her. She begins to grow like the garden and fly like the birds.

Suppose you met a bird who did for you what Mary's robin does for her. This bird will offer you a way to find out who you truly are. It will also lead you to a place where you can grow and prosper. Think about this; then answer the questions below.

1. a. What kind of bird will you meet? Why did you choose this type?

   _____
   _____
   _____

   b. Why do you suppose Francis Hodgson Burnett chose a robin for Mary?

   _____
   _____
   _____

2. What will the bird do for you to help you find out who you are?

   _____
   _____
   _____

3. Where will the bird take you so that you can grow and prosper?

   _____
   _____
   _____

Name: _____ Date: _____

Trust

Part of feeling free is being able to trust others and your surroundings. When you are confident that those around you will respect your boundaries, space, and confidences, then you are free to grow as well as to share with the others who you truly are. As Mary Lennox begins to trust others, she also begins to find out who she really is.

For each of the characters below, write down the reason(s) why Mary trusts him or her.

Character	Reasons
1. Dickon	
2. Colin	
3. Martha	
4. Ben Weatherstaff	
5. Susan Sowerby	

Respond:

1. Of all these characters, who would you most trust? Why?

   _____

   _____

2. Are you trustworthy? Explain.

   _____

   _____

Name: _____ Date: _____

"I Can Live Forever!"

When Colin enters the secret garden, he is compelled to call out, "I can live forever!" As the author describes, he is experiencing one of those rare and precious moments when a human being feels that he or she can live forever. These moments cannot be planned, but rather, a person will be surprised by them when he or she is feeling particularly in tune with nature and the world around him or her. The author suggests that certain sunrises or sunsets can produce this feeling. Colin, of course, finds it in simply being out in a growing, thriving, natural place.

Reread the section of the book in which Colin declares he can live forever. Also read again the author's explanation of that feeling. Has there ever been a time in your life when you felt this way? Think about it. In the space below, describe the experience and your feelings. Paint a picture with words so that others might know how you felt and what brought the feeling about.

_____

_____

_____

_____

_____

_____

_____

_____

_____

_____

_____

_____

Journey

by Patricia MacLachlan (Delacorte Press, 1991)

(Available in Canada, Delacorte; UK, Delacorte; Australia, Transworld Publishers)

Summary: In one of the most beautifully moving young adult novels of recent history, Patricia MacLachlan, author of the award-winning *Sarah, Plain and Tall,* tells the story of Journey, a young boy searching for his history, family, and sense of belonging.

Journey and his sister, Cat, have always lived with their grandparents, Lottie and Marcus, as well as their mother, Liddie. Yet, Liddie is restless. Once she seemed contented at home with her husband and children, but since the time her spouse left years before, it has become evident that Liddie is not content to remain in "the here and now." She wants to keep searching; she always looks for what will happen next. One day, she packs her things, and telling the children that she will send for them, she moves away with no forwarding address. Cat, Lottie, and Marcus are not surprised by her departure, and they know she will not be back nor will she send for the children. But Journey hopes. He cannot bear to blame his mother, for this would, in some way, be an acceptance of the truth. Instead, his insides ache with anger, loneliness, and feelings of abandonment.

Yet, Journey's painful feelings are countered by the framework of family love and warmth in which he lives. His grandparents are clearly attached to one another as well as to their grandchildren. They also model for Journey how to live with a strong sense of self, pursuing their daily pleasures and fulfilling their creative needs. Grandma reads, gardens, and is learning to play the flute. Grandfather is charmed by photography.

It is through the use of his camera that Marcus truly does help Journey. He begins to take photographs of the family and its members, as well as their friends and the farm on which they live. He posts these photos up on the barn walls, and eventually Journey himself catches the fever and takes photos, too. He begins to see things in the photographs, things he did not notice before. He even sees an old photograph of his mother as a girl, and he cannot deny her lack of attachment to other people in the scene. The reality of her inability to connect with others is brought to him, literally, in black and white.

Journey also discovers that his mother has destroyed all of their family photos. She has ripped them up in an act that Cat calls a murder. His grandfather, however, finds the negatives, and he secretly builds a dark room to develop them. Journey sees the images he has been longing to see. But more importantly, he remembers what he has been longing to remember. It was his grandfather, all along, who loved and cared for him. It was his grandfather who gave him a home, a family, and a history. Journey has found that for which he was searching.

Name: _____ Date: _____

Pictures of You

If you have photographs available, find one of you as a very young child, another of you in the middle of your life, and a current one of you. Affix each to the top of a sheet of paper. (You can do so without permanently attaching the photographs by using the photo corners available at most stores selling photographic supplies.) Under each picture, write what that picture says about you at that time. Write without thinking about whether or not you are writing an accurate description.

Now look at the photographs and at what you have written. Do you think that pictures "show us what is really there," or do you think, "Sometimes the truth is somewhere behind the pictures"? Respond here.

Name: _____ Date: _____

Learning From Others

Sometimes we learn the most about ourselves from other people. Tell something that Journey learns about himself from each of the characters named below. Explain your response with evidence from the book.

1. Marcus

_____

_____

2. Lottie

_____

_____

3. Cat

_____

_____

4. Bloom

_____

_____

5. Cooper

_____

_____

6. Mr. McDougall

_____

_____

7. Emmett

_____

_____

Respond:

Who in your life has taught you the most about yourself? Explain.

_____

_____

_____

Name: _____ Date: _____

The Importance of Names

Most authors are very careful about the names they choose for their characters. The names seem to support and even shed light on who that character is. Patricia Maclachlan seems particularly selective in her novel, *Journey*. The names are quite suggestive of certain traits within the individuals. Think about each of the names; then next to each, write what you think the name says about the person.

1. Journey

_____

_____

2. Lottie

_____

_____

3. Marcus

_____

_____

4. Cat

_____

_____

5. Bloom

_____

_____

Respond:

1. Does your name say something about you? If so, explain what it says here. If not, what name would say something about you? Write that name here and explain what it says.

_____

_____

2. What other book have you read where a character's name really said something about that character? What is the name? What did it say about him/her?

_____

_____

Name: _____ Date: _____

The Importance of Names, Part II

Look over the list of words below. Just as "journey" is a common word that happens to make a good name for the main character of the story, which of the words below would make a good name for you? Circle or highlight each that appeals to you, and after it write a brief reason why.

- amber
- angel
- autumn
- azure
- blaze
- comet
- coral
- crystal
- diamond
- eagle
- ebony
- flower
- freedom
- ivory
- joy
- jump
- leaf
- light
- love
- magic
- midnight
- moon
- mouse

- peace
- play
- rainbow
- river
- rose
- ruby
- satin
- sky
- smoke
- snake
- spring
- star
- stone
- storm
- summer
- sunrise
- sunset
- tiger
- velvet
- wind
- winter
- wolf

Name: _____ Date: _____

A Kiss to Remember It By

Once when his grandfather laughs, Journey kisses him to seal the memory. The laughter is precious to him, and he wants to celebrate and hold on to it. He creates a moment, something he can keep and treasure forever.

Some people say that if you press your thumb and index finger together during a special moment, you will create an "anchor" that can draw that *feeling memory* back to you whenever you want it. The same would be true if you pulled on your ear lobe or pinched the back of your hand. Whenever you pinched your hand again, you would remember.

Sometimes smells are good reminders. It is said that the sense of smell has the best memory. For example, if your mother wore a certain perfume when you were a baby, chances are that if you happened to smell that perfume today, the feelings of being a baby and the sense of your mother during that time would come back to you.

Regardless of how you remember, every individual has some special memories that are frozen in time, ready to come back at a moment's notice. What are your precious memories? Do some brainstorming, and jot down the memories that come to you immediately.

_____   _____

_____   _____

_____   _____

Now, from your list choose a memory that is very significant for you. What makes you think of that memory? A photograph? A person? A smell? A season? Write about the memory here, beginning with the word, "Whenever . . ." Continue with your memory anchor, like "Whenever I smell the ocean . . .," or, "Whenever I see my friend Chris . . ." If you would like, share your memory with the class. You may also keep the memory just for yourself if you would prefer.

Memory

Whenever . . .

_____

_____

_____

_____

_____

_____

Name: _____ Date: _____

Showing Feelings

Each of the main characters has feelings about Liddie's departure. The author tells us some of those feelings directly. Others we assume or guess from what the characters say and how they behave. What do each of the following characters feel about the loss of Liddie and the effects of her leaving? Write both the feeling and how you know.

1. Journey

_____

_____

_____

2. Cat

_____

_____

_____

3. Lottie

_____

_____

_____

4. Marcus

_____

_____

_____

Respond:

Think about the last thing that happened to you about which you had strong feelings. What happened? What were your feelings? Did other people know your feelings? What did you do to show them or to avoid showing them?

_____

_____

_____

_____

Name: _____ Date: _____

A Way to Save That Sound

When Journey takes a photograph of his grandfather and Emmett playing together, he wants to capture the sounds that Emmett makes just as he captures the image of the two people. In today's world, we capture sound all the time on audio tape. Can you think of any other ways to save sound? In small groups or as a class, brainstorm for ways, to capture sounds without taping them.

Now, take a few minutes to jot down some of your favorite sounds. (Here are a few ideas to get you thinking: the ocean, laughter, motorcycle engines, birds chirping, water rippling, cats purring.)

Choose one of the sounds from your list. "Capture" that sound for the class by describing it here. Paint it with words, so that as they read or listen, others can actually "hear" the sound you are describing. Use words that make sounds themselves, like "buzz," "whir," "roar," and so forth.

To Capture a Sound

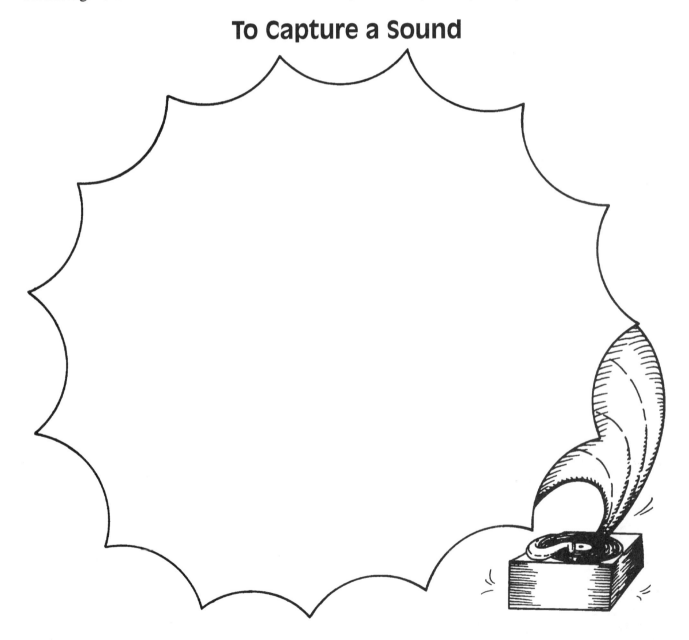

Name: _____ Date: _____

Family Albums

In looking through family portraits, it becomes clear that Cat not only resembles her mother, but she bears a striking resemblance to her grandmother as well. Likewise, she takes after her grandmother in personality. Journey, he is shocked to discover, is almost a physical duplicate of his grandfather, and as Cat says, they are two of a kind.

If family portraits are available to you, take a look through the pictures of your immediate and extended families. Now respond to the following questions. (**Note to the teacher:** Please see page 176.)

1. Do you notice any persons with resemblances to yourself? Who?

2. Do you notice things that you and others have in common in the way of manner and dress?

3. Is there anyone in your family that others are always saying you "take after"?

4. How do you feel about these resemblances?

5. If you could choose to resemble someone in your family, who would it be and why?

Name: _____ Date: _____

Blame and Acceptance

"You need someone to blame, Journey?" his grandfather asks him, and the answer would have been, "Yes," had Journey spoken. He wants to blame someone, but blaming his mother would cause him too much pain. That would mean he had to accept the fact that she abandoned him. The need to blame someone keeps Journey stuck in his feelings. Acceptance of the truth helps him to let go and move forward.

Most people wish to avoid pain. Oftentimes, people will seek out someone to blame in order to make themselves feel better. They do not have to hurt about the loss or difficulty as long as they can hang on to resentment and indignation. The problem is that blame keeps a person frozen. Acceptance of the situation, getting into the solution, as it were, sets a person free.

Read over each blaming statement given below. Following each, write a new way of looking at the situation that can help a person move out of the blame and into acceptance (that is, out of the problem and into the solution).

1. "It's the government's fault that there are so many homeless people."

2. "It's the schools' fault that students drop out before graduating."

3. "It's the police department's fault that there is so much crime in our neighborhoods."

4. "It's the parents' fault that many students don't do their homework or come to school every day."

5. "It's _____ fault that _____." (Fill in the previous blanks with a blaming statement that you hear frequently. Respond to it just as you have with the others.)

Unit Award

Use the award below as a celebration of freedom. It can function as a certificate, a cover sheet, a classroom decoration, or anything you would like.

In Celebration of Freedom
This Certificate
Recognizes

_____

Bibliography

The following bibliography suggests additional works of fiction and nonfiction that are worthwhile reading under the theme "Freedom." This list is only a sampling, and it is by no means comprehensive.

FICTION

Axline, Virginia M. *Dibs in Search of Self.* Ballantine, 1964.

Baylor, Byrd. *Hawk, I'm Your Brother.* Scribner, 1976.

Clark, Margeret. *Freedom Crossing.* Scholastic, Inc., 1989.

Freedman, Russell. *Buffalo Hunt.* Holiday House, 1988.

Fritz, Jean. *China Homecoming.* Putnam, 1985.

George, Jean Craighead. *Julie of the Wolves.* HarperCollins, 1974.

George, Jean Craighead. *On the Far Side of the Mountain.* Dutton, 1990.

Haley, Alex. *Roots.* Arrow Books, 1985.

Hanson, Joyce. *Out from This Place.* Avon, 1992.

Hungry Wolf, Beverly. *The Ways of My Grandmothers.* Quill, 1980.

Jeffers, Susan (Illustrator). *Brother Eagle, Sister Sky: A Message from Chief Seattle.* Dial, 1991.

Jenkins, Lyll Becerrada. *Honorable Prison.* Penguin, 1989.

L'Engle, Madeleine. *A Ring of Endless Light.* Farrar, Straus, & Giroux, 1980.

Lester, Julius. *To Be a Slave.* Dial, 1968.

Levine, Ellen. *Freedom's Children.* Putnam Pub. Group, 1993.

London, Jack. *The Call of the Wild.* Macmillan, 1963.

Lord, Betty Bao. *In the Year of the Boar and Jackie Robinson.* Harper, 1984.

O'Dell, Scott. *Sing Down the Moon.* Houghton Mifflin, 1970.

Peck, Robert Newton. *A Day No Pigs Would Die.* Dell, 1979.

Rawls, Wilson. *Where the Red Fern Grows.* Bantam, 1974.

Speare, Elizabeth George. *The Witch of Blackbird Pond.* Houghton, 1958.

Spinelli, Jerry. *Maniac Magee.* Little, Brown, & Co., 1990.

Taylor, Mildred. *The Friendship.* Dial, 1987.

Twain, Mark. *The Adventures of Huckelberry Finn.* Bantam, 1981.

Uchida, Yoshiko. *Journey Home.* Macmillan, 1978.

Unwin, Nora. *Amos Fortune: Free Man.* Dutton, 1967.

Whiteley, Opal. *Opal: The Journal of an Understanding Heart.* Tioga Publishing, 1984.

Yep, Laurence. *The Rainbow People.* HarperCollins, 1989.

NONFICTION

Chaikin, Miriam. *Nightmare in History: The Holocaust, 1931–1945.* Clarion, 1987.

Clayton, Edward T. *Martin Luther King: The Peaceful Warrior.* Archway, 1968.

Darby, Jean. *Martin Luther King, Jr.* Lerner, 1990.

Denenberg, Barry. *Nelson Mandela: No Easy Walk to Freedom.* Scholastic, 1991.

Evitts, William J. *Captive Bodies, Free Spirits: The Story of Southern Slavery.* Messner, 1985.

Fisher, Leonard Everett. *All Times, All People: A World History of Slavery.* Harper, 1980.

Freedman, Russell. *Indian Chiefs.* Holiday House, 1987.

Hamilton, Veronica. *W.E.B. Du Bois: A Biography.* Harper, 1972.

Kosoff, Anna. *The Civil Rights Movement and Its Legacy.* Franklin Watts, 1989.

Moore, Yvette. *Freedom Songs.* Orchard, 1991.

Taylor, C.L. *Censorship.* Watts, 1986.

Answer Key

If answers for a page are not given, then the questions or problems on that page are, to some degree, subjective. Students' answers on such pages will vary.

Page 12: Algebra

1. x = 23
2. x = 8
3. x = 82
4. x = 62
5. x = 1
6. x = 0
7. x = 990
8. x = 7
9. x = 23
10. x = 248

Page 13: Logic

Age	First House	Second House	Third House	Fourth House	Fifth House	Sixth House
One	Zachary					
Two			Brianna			
Three						Travis
Four					Kenny	
Five				Alicia		
Six		Nicholas				

Page 36: Motion Wordsearch

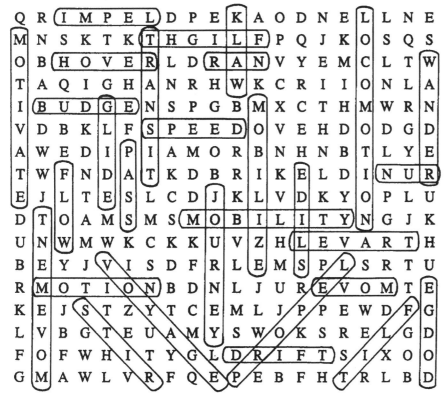

Answer Key *(cont.)*

Page 39: Travel Equations

1. 330 miles (528.2 km)
2. Answers will vary.
3. A. 444 miles (710.4 km)
4. 254 miles (406.4 km)
5. approximately 4.2 hours
6. approximately 6 hours and 45 minutes
7. approximately 3 hours
8. 1,394,550 square miles (3,570,480 sq. km)
9. Buffalo to Amarillo = 4 hours and 15 minutes
   Amarillo to Seattle = 4 hours and 15 minutes
   Seattle to Buffalo = 6 hours and 45 minutes
10. yes

Page 78: Percentages

1. 6,000 people
2. 4,500 people
3. 37.5%
4. 9,600 people
5. 5500 voters
6. 3,762 people
7. 28%
8. 1,375 voters
9. 25%
10. 1,026 people
11. 67% (rounded)
12. 12% (rounded)

Page 79: Genetics

1. no
2. 1 in 4
3. TT or TN
4. two blue-eyed alleles
5. D = dark hair; B = blond hair

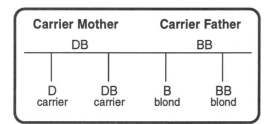

Page 86: How to Become President of the United States

1. yes
2. yes
3. yes
4. no
5. yes
6. no
7. no (in 1994)
8. no
9. yes
10. most likely no

Page 113: Paying Bills

Amount enclosed = $53.84

1. the call to London, ONT
2. the toll calls
3. Green Bay Phone Company
   P.O. Box 11
   Green Bay, WI 59230

Page 131: Judaism

1. ancient people from whom the Jews descended
2. spiritual teacher and leader; interpreter of Jewish law
3. writings that act as a guide to Jewish law; also tell of Jewish history and folklore
4. first five books of the Hebrew Bible ("Old Testament")
5. Jewish prayer book
6. first ancestor of the Jewish people; one of the three patriarchs of the Jews
7. Abraham's wife; one of the four matriarchs of the Jews
8. Abraham's son; one of the three patriarchs
9. Isaac's wife; one of the four matriarchs
10. Isaac's son; one of the three patriarchs
11. Jacob's wife; one of the four matriarchs
12. Jacob's wife; one of the four matriarchs
13. Jewish New Year, celebrating the creation of the world and God's rule
14. Day of Atonement; day of prayer, thoughtful regret for past wrongs, and hope for future good deeds
15. celebration of the Jews' escape from slavery in Egypt

Answer Key *(cont.)*

Page 131: Judaism *(cont.)*

16. celebration of the gift of the Torah to the Jews
17. Harvest Festival
18. Feast of Lights, celebrating Jewish freedom from the Syrians
19. God's law as given to Moses
20. Jewish house of worship; place for Jewish education and community activity
21. seventh day of the Jewish week (Saturday), a holy day of rest
22. skullcap worn in reverence to God
23. Israelite escape from slavery in Egypt
24. Kingdom of Israel
25. land where Abraham settled (approximately between 1800 and 1500 B.C.)

Page 156: Flowers

1. shrub with green branches; often leafless; showy, yellow flowers like butterflies (pea family)
2. grasslike leaves; white, yellow, and purple flowers made of six nearly equal petals; blossom shaped like upside-down teardrop; very small plant (iris family)
3. yellow flower with trumpetlike center and 5 or 6 petals that flare to the sides; one blossom at the end of each green stalk; 5-6 bluish-green leaves on stalk (amaryllis family)
4. spiny evergreen shrub with yellow flowers; many dark green branches; fragrant (also called "furze" or "whim") (pea family)
5. low, evergreen shrub; broomlike branches; scaly leaves like needles; hairy stalk; purple-pink flowers shaped like bells (heath family)
6. two or three large, oblong leaves; cluster of tiny, white, bell-shaped flowers off a green stem (lily family)
7. fernlike leaves; yellow, orange, or red-brown blossoms made of many petals (resembling the frilly edge of a flamenco dancer's skirt); strong odor; hardy (composite family)
8. fragrant; delicate blossoms of yellow, white, or pink; six petals surrounding a short or long trumpet; sword-shaped leaves (amaryllis family)
9. many shades of pink, yellow, red, and white; large or small blossoms; often thorns on stem; many varieties; flowers usually unfold to layers of petals (rose family)
10. colorful; hardy; each blossom has two petals that open like jaws when pressed on the sides; velvety; plant can grow up to 3 feet (90 cm); blossoms grow off the same stalk, rising from larger blossoms in full bloom to smaller ones just budding (figwort family)
11. delicate, white blossom made of 3 or so petals; flower seems made of snow; 2 or 3 narrow, green leaves growing straight from the bulb; one stem from bulb with one bell-shaped flower at top; flower nods downward (amaryllis family)
12. sharp spines and prickly leaves; silky flowers of purple or purple-pink; round heads later form downy balls of seed that blow away like a dandelion (composite family)

Page 170: Family Albums

Remember that some students may not have any family portraits available due to a variety of personal, social, and cultural reasons. Also, adopted children may not bear a resemblance to their family members.